Custom
COUTURE

32 ways to transform your wardrobe with needle and thread

HÉLÈNE LE BERRE

sixth&spring books

NEW YORK, NY

Editorial director: Christophe Savouré
Editor: Christine Hooghe, assisted by Charlotte Walckenaer
Creative director: Laurent Quellet
Art director: Julie Pauwels
Layout: Vanessa Paris
Photography: Frédéric Lucano
Stylist: Lélia Deshayes
Models: Aga Alchimowicz and Élodie Zangaris
Technical illustrations: Iwona Séris
Garment illustrations: Émilie Ramon
Contributor: Marie Pieroni
Samplemaking: Florence Bellot and Sophie Lequesne

Acknowledgments

3SUISSES.fr

The publisher and author thank 3 Suisses
for providing all the garments
customized in these pages.
Online catalog: www.3suisses.fr
Information: 0892 69 15 00

A huge thank you also to:

La Droguerie
9, 11 rue du Jour, 75001 PARIS
01 45 08 93 27
www.ladroguerie.com

Pain d'Épices
29, 31, 33 Passage Jouffroy, 75009 PARIS
01 47 70 08 68
www.paindepices.fr

Carole et Manuel who opened
their apartment for photography.

The painting in the photographs on pages 112, 119 and 136
is the work of Claire Basler.
For more information about the work of the artist:
c.basler@orange.fr / 06 75 87 31 38 / www.claire-basler.com

sixth&springbooks

First published in the United States in 2011 by
Sixth&Spring Books
161 Avenue of the Americas
New York, NY 10013
www.sixthandspringbooks.com

Library of Congress Control Number: 2010939372
ISBN 13: 978-1-936096-16-9

First published in France as *Tendance Vintage* by Groupe Fleurus
15/27 rue Moussorgski
75895 Paris Cedex 18

© Groupe Fleurus—Paris, 2007

Manufactured in China
1 3 5 7 9 10 8 6 4 2

First English Edition
© 2011 by Sixth and Spring Books
For more information about the work of the artist:
c.basler@orange.fr / 06 75 87 31 38 / www.claire-basler.com

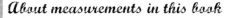

About measurements in this book

Inches or centimeters? The measurement equivalents in this book have been calculated on a
case-by-case basis to make your work easy. For each project, choose one system and follow it consistently.

For my sister

What young girl hasn't dreamed of creating marvelous clothes to wear? If you've picked up this book and read this far, chances are you, too, have dreamed of becoming a fashion designer—accumulating all those scraps of fabric, bits of ribbon, buttons and beads along the way. In these pages you'll find that you can create unique fashions by embellishing just a few ready-to-wear basics.

Look through your closet for items that could be modified. Be inspired: search the remnants at the fabric store. Take up your scissors and needles! Don't hesitate to cut up, take apart or add details to existing clothes: even little changes can completely alter the look and bring out your personality. The minute you begin, you are a designer!

Contents

Boho

Jet Set

Retro

Diva

Charmingly trimmed
Does a plain, dark tank top strike you as dull? Turn it into a terrific top by finishing the bottom edge with a border of Art Nouveau–print fabric and some easy, delicate bead embroidery. Add some dangling ties trimmed with fabric yo-yos to one strap— that's all it takes!
Instructions p. 24

9

Button artistry
To give some style to
a pullover blouse,
outline a faux yoke
with a strip of fabric,
then fill the area
with a scattering of
assorted buttons and
tiny embroidered
knots. It will make
you smile....
Instructions p. 26

10

Breezy skirt

Here's a skirt that invites a cool mix of colors and fabrics! Worked wrong-side out, it is bordered with a faux flounce made of three pleated bands of fabric. Trim it with felted wool accents and add sequins for the final touch.
Instructions p. 28

Fit to be tied

At once chic and fresh
with its bubble hem,
this top is simply
a plain tank draped with
additional fabric. It
makes news with a big
bow with long tails
edged in jet-black beads.
It's great to wear during
the day, but you'll love
this look at night, too.
Instructions p. 30

15

Flower power

An origami technique adds a clever twist to this wrap-front sweater. Replace the lower sleeves with a sweet floral fabric and trim the join with a pleated band. To top it off, embroider over some of the floral motifs. This one is very fun to make.
Instructions p. 32

17

Folk cardigan
Give new life to a favorite black cable pullover by slashing the front in two! Next, bind the edges with a brightly colored fabric and add a flirty bow at the neckline. Then decorate the sweater with freehand embroidery that accents whatever the knitted pattern may be.
Instructions p. 38

Gypsy chic

Is it possible to add a sophisticated touch to a peasant blouse? Yes! Simply sew on a row of fabric-covered beads so they outline the yoke, then embroider lines of French knots over the striped background using silver thread.
Instructions p. 36

20

In the red

Don't let winter make a fashion victim of you. Here's a simple way to dress up a classic coat: trim it with appliqués in a manner that brings out the lines of the garment, add tiny silk ribbon flowers . . . and change the buttons!
Instructions p. 41

23

Charmingly trimmed

 From the closet
Dark brown tank top with skinny straps, not snug around the hips

Tip
You can adapt this project to hide a worn area at the bottom of the tank top or cover a motif you don't like. To do this, calculate the height of the bottom band as needed to cover the area plus 1" (2.5 cm).

1. Prepare the fabric
Try on the tank top and measure around your hips; add ¾" (2 cm); the result = L. On the wrong side of the Art Nouveau fabric, mark a band L x 3" (7 cm), being sure to center the motifs pleasingly. Cut it out. Lay the band wrong-side up on your ironing board, and, pressing each fold with the iron as you go, turn up ¼" (0.5 cm) along the top edge, and then ⅜" (1 cm) at each end. Along the bottom edge, turn up ¼" (0.5 cm) and then ½" (1.5 cm).

2. Apply the border
Mark a line parallel to and 2" (4.5 cm) above the bottom all around the tank. Starting and ending at one side seam and aligning the top of the band with the marked line, pin the top of the band to the tank. Tuck the bottom of the tank into the bottom fold of the band and pin. Using a whipstitch, sew the top of the band to the outside of the tank, the bottom of the band to the inside, and the ends to each other.

MATERIALS
- Art Nouveau–print fabric, 44" x 8" (110 x 20 cm): lavender, beige and blue on white
- Print fabric, 11" x ¾" (27 x 2 cm): blue on beige
- Small rocaille (tube) beads: shiny light pink
- Sewing thread: lavender, beige
- Pearl cotton, size 5 or 8: red
- Lightweight cardboard

SUPPLIES
- Basic sewing supplies (see page 149)
- Embroidery needle
- Compass

Refer to the basic techniques on pages 150–153

24

3. Embroider the bead motifs

Beginning at the top of the appliquéd band, mark vertical guidelines 2½" (6 cm) high at regular intervals around the tank top (if possible, align each with the center of a motif on the band).

Referring to the photo and using doubled lavender thread, sew eleven beads along one of the marked lines. On each side of this, about ¼" (0.5 cm) away, sew a line of five beads, then another of 2 beads. For the best results, sew the lines one at a time, knotting the thread on the wrong side at each end. Repeat to sew a group of five beaded lines at each marked guideline.

4. Make the dangling trims

From the Art Nouveau fabric, cut two strips, each 3½" x ¾" (9 x 2 cm). Also cut three strips this size from the other print fabric. Using the iron, press a narrow margin to the wrong side on each edge of each strip. Then fold each strip in half lengthwise, right-side out. Using an overcast stitch and the pearl cotton or beige sewing thread, sew the open edges of each strip closed.

Draw a circle 1⅜" (3.5 cm) in diameter on the cardboard. Cut this out for a template, then trace around it six times on the wrong side of the Art Nouveau fabric. Cut out the circles. Referring to page 153 and using the iron, fold and press a narrow margin to the wrong side around each circle. Then, with doubled lavender thread, sew a running stitch along the edge all around. Pull the thread to gather the fabric as tightly as possible, then knot and cut the thread. Flatten the yo-yos so the gathers are in the center of one side. Sew a yo-yo to each end of each strip.

Fold the strips in half as shown. Refer to the photos to pin the strips to the tank; then sew them on with small stitches.

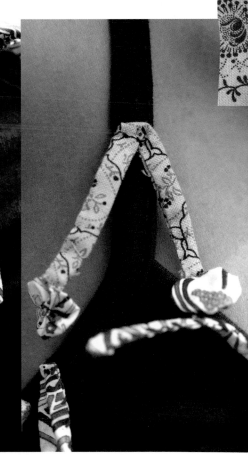

Button artistry

MATERIALS
+ Print fabric, 36" x ¾"
(90 x 2 cm): plum on tea color
+ An assortment of playful
buttons: mostly red
+ Sewing thread: ecru
+ Pearl cotton, size 5 or 8: red

SUPPLIES
+ Basic sewing supplies
(see page 149)
+ Embroidery needle

Refer to the basic
techniques on pages
150–153

 From the closet

Blue-and-white striped pullover blouse with small standing collar

Tip

Arrange the buttons on the shirt in a way you like. Then take a photo so you have something to refer to and don't have to worry about which goes where as you sew them on.

1. Outline the shirtfront

Photocopy the pattern on page 154, enlarging to 150%, and cut it out. Pin it to the front of the shirt, placing the top edge at the bottom of the collar. Mark the perimeter on the shirt, then remove the pattern. On each side, extend the vertical marks up to the shoulder seam. Measure the marked outline from shoulder to shoulder; this length plus 1¼" (3 cm) = L.

2. Add the border

Cut a strip of print fabric L x ¾" (2 cm). Lay the strip wrong-side up on your ironing board, and, pressing each fold with your iron as you go, turn ¼" (0.5 cm) up along each long edge. Beginning at one shoulder seam (leave a bit extending toward the back) pin the strip right-side-up to the yoke, aligning it to the inside of the marked guide. To fit it to the curves, fold tiny darts into the strip as you pin. Fold the end of the strip under at each shoulder seam. Whipstitch all four edges of the strip to the shirt.

3. Add your buttons!

Arrange the buttons on the yoke area in a way you like. Mark the placement of each with a chalk or pencil dot at its center. Using pearl cotton, sew the buttons on one at a time, knotting and cutting the thread after attaching each one.

4. Embroider decorative knots

Add embroidered knots in between the buttons. For each, thread a needle with pearl cotton but don't knot the end. Insert the needle from the right side and bring it out again about ⅛" (0.2 cm) away, leaving a tail about ¾" (2 cm) long at the beginning. Make three backstitches in the same place (**drawings 1 and 2**). Cut both ends of the thread about ¼" (0.5 cm) above the fabric.

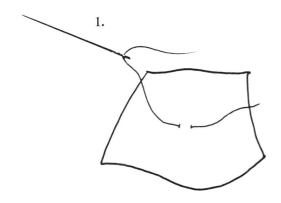

1.

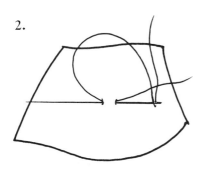

2.

27

Breezy skirt

 From the closet

Flared, below-knee-length skirt, preferably with godets at the hemline; floral print on black

Tip

In order to mute the colors, this skirt is used wrong-side out. Since the seams show, trim any thread ends close to the surface … and cut off any labels! If your skirt is very full, you may need more fabric bands to circle the bottom.

1. Make the faux flounce

Mark ten bands, each 2¼" (5 cm) high, all across the wrong side of the fabric. Cut them out. Lay each wrong-side-up on your ironing board, and, pressing each fold with your iron as you go, turn ½" (1 cm) up along each long edge.

With the right sides together and opening the folds as you go, pin and sew the bands together, end-to-end, to make one long band; use a narrow seam allowance. Starting at one end, pin a tiny pleat into the top edge of the band every 4" (10 cm) (drawing 1). Topstitch close to the long edges.

Turn the skirt wrong-side out. Overlap the pleated edge of the band, right-side up, on the bottom edge of the skirt (use a very narrow overlap and keep the work flat so the skirt edge doesn't gather up). Pin the band in place. When you've gone all around, cut the band, leaving a little excess, and lap one end over the other, folding it under. Baste the band to the skirt and then sew close to the pleated edge.

In the same way, apply two more bands (**drawing 2**); **don't worry about aligning the pleats.**

MATERIALS

- Floral print fabric with gray striped background, 44" x 20" (110 x 50 cm)
- Wool roving: white, bright red, cranberry, sky blue, yellow
- Sequins, size 0.5 cm (center hole): fuchsia, iridescent pale pink, yellow
- Sequins, size 1 cm (off-center hole): transparent pink
- Sewing thread: gray
- Pearl cotton, size 5 or 8: black

SUPPLIES

- Basic sewing supplies (see page 149)
- Sewing machine
- Felting needle
- Styrofoam block for felting
- Embroidery needle

Refer to the basic techniques on pages 150–153

28

1.

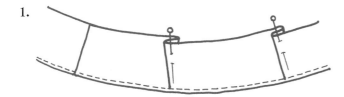

2.

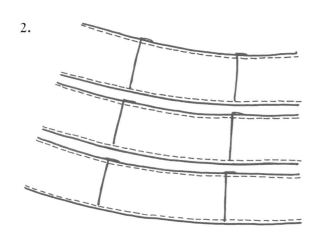

2. Add felted piping

Slide the foam block inside the skirt, under the seam between the top and middle bands. Moving the block along the seam as you go, needle-felt the white roving onto the seam. Work all around then decorate the lower seam in the same way.

3. Add felted motifs

The seamlines of the godets in the skirt establish the areas to embellish. If your skirt doesn't have godets, mark triangles 5" (12 cm) wide and 6" (15 cm) high at regular intervals around the original hemline—just above the added bands.

Slide the foam block inside the skirt, under a godet (or triangle). Needle-felt oversize leaf or flower shapes randomly on the godet, mixing the colors of wool roving for effect. In the same way, embellish every alternate godet or triangle.

4. The final touch: paillettes!

Using pearl cotton and the overcast stitch, sew the paillettes to the seam allowances of the embellished godets (or along the triangle edges). Use the different sizes and colors randomly.

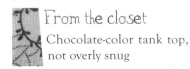

Fit to be tied

From the closet
Chocolate-color tank top,
not overly snug

Tips
• To calculate the length to cut the bubble top, measure the tank top from just below the armhole to the bottom edge and add 16" (40.5 cm). Check this length before before purchasing your fabric.
• To keep the tank stretched to the right size while sewing the bubble in place, insert a piece of cardboard half the width of your high-bust measurement (breathe deep to measure).

1. Add the bubble to the tank top
Sew the bubble
Fold the green and yellow print fabric in half, wrong-side out, aligning the short edges. Pin or baste the short edges together; then sew by machine, leaving ¼" (0.5 cm) seam allowance.

Pressing the folds with an iron as you go, turn ¼" (0.5 cm) and then ½" (1.5 cm) to the wrong side along the bottom edge. Sew the hem close to the first fold.

On the top edge, turn 1" (2.5 cm) to the wrong side and press the fold.

Gather the top edge

Attach the bubble
On the right side of the tank top, mark a horizontal line all around, 1¼" (3 cm) below the armholes. Slide the tank over

MATERIALS
• Print fabric, 52" x 18" (130 x 45 cm): green and yellow on chocolate
• Polka-dot fabric, 40" x 3¼" (100 x 8 cm): white on aqua
• Small rocaille (tube) beads: shiny black
• Round elastic,1 yard (90 cm)
• Sewing thread: black, aqua

SUPPLIES
• Basic sewing supplies (see page 149)
• Sewing machine
• Safety pin
• Seam ripper

Refer to the basic techniques on pages 150–153

a chair back (or the cardboard noted at left) to keep it stretched while you add the bubble. (This is important for ensuring that the finished garment will have enough stretch for you to put it on.) Slide the bubble tube over the tank, placing the seam at one side seam. Align the top edge with the marked guideline; pin. Using an open backstitch, sew through all layers, stitching close to the gathering thread.

Add the elastic to the hem
Open the side seam in the bottom hem of the bubble tube. Affix the elastic in the safety pin and thread it through the hem. Knot the elastic ends together; slide the knot into the hem. Re-sew the side seam by hand.

2. Make the bow

Fold the polka-dot fabric in half lengthwise, wrong-side out. Leaving an opening for turning in the middle of the long edge and pivoting to create a 45° angle at each end, sew ¼" (0.5 cm) from the cut edge; trim the points (**drawing 1**). Turn the strip right-side-out. Sew the opening closed by hand. Tie the strip into a bow, arranging the loops and tails evenly.

Thread a needle with black thread; affix in the point of one tail. Slide three beads over the needle onto the thread. Take one overcast stitch over the edge. Repeat to outline the entire bow with beads (**drawing 2**). Each time you reach the bow knot (or if you need to rethread the needle), secure your work with a few stitches without beads.

Sew the bow to the center front of the tank top by hand, placing it just below the gathers at the top of the bubble and stitching through all layers.

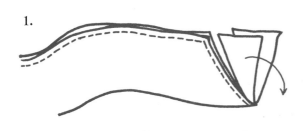

1.

2.

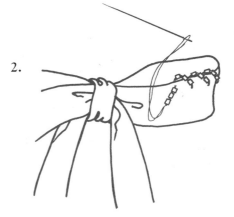

Flower power

From the closet

Pink, lightweight lacy wrap-front sweater with long sleeves

MATERIALS
• Floral print fabric, 45" x 18"
(110 x 45 cm): pink on white
• Sewing thread: pink
• Tapestry wool: fuchsia,
lavender, light pink
• Cardboard: approximately
10" x 4" (25 x 10 cm)

SUPPLIES
• Basic sewing supplies
(see page 149)
• Sewing machine
• Large embroidery
needle

**Refer to the basic
techniques on pages
150–153**

Tip
For the origami-pleated trim at the biceps, you need a fabric strip three times as long as the finished trim should be. Be sure to allow extra at the strip ends.

1. Create the oversleeves
Sew the oversleeves
Lay the sweater flat. Across each sleeve, mark a line 7" (18 cm) below the bodice shoulder seam; if possible, mark along a row of knit stitches. This line must be at least 1¼" (3 cm) below the armhole (**drawing 1**). Measure the line just marked; double this length = T.

On the wrong side of the floral fabric, draw two trapezoids as shown in **drawing 2**. Check that the length is right for you: the fabric should create a three-quarter-length sleeve once it is attached to the line marked on the sweater sleeve. For seam allowances, add ¼" (1 cm) to the top and sides, and 2" (5 cm) at the bottom; shape the contours as shown. Cut out the oversleeves.

Fold each oversleeve in half lengthwise, wrong-side out. Baste and then sew along the seamline, following the angles as shown (**drawing 3**). Pressing the folds with an iron as you go, turn ¼" (0.5 cm) and then 1¾" (4 cm) to the wrong side along the bottom edge. Pin, then sew the hem with invisible stitches. At the top of each sleeve, fold and press ¼" (1 cm) to the wrong side. Turn the oversleeves right-side out.

Attach the oversleeves
Cut the cardboad to a width equal to T divided by two. Slide it into one of the sweater sleeves. Slide one of the fabric oversleeves onto the sweater sleeve. Align the underarm seams and place the top of the oversleeve on the marked guideline. Pin, then whipstitch the oversleeve to the sweater. Attach the other oversleeve in the same way.

Roll up the oversleeves and pin out of the way. Cut off the sweater sleeves about ½" (1.5 cm) below the seam. Overcast the cut edge by hand with doubled thread.

1.

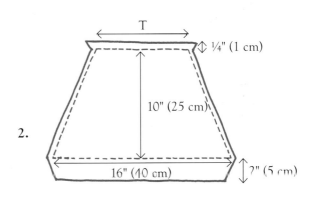

2.

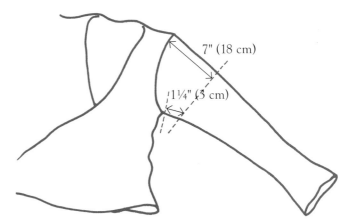

3.

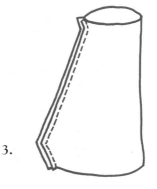

33

Flower power *continued*

2. Origami pleated trim

Cut two bands of floral fabric 44" x 3" (110 x 7 cm). Lay each wrong-side up and fold the long edges over to the center, overlapping slightly so the width is 1¼" (3 cm).

Turn one band over. Make a triangle 1¾" (4 cm) from the right-hand end as follows: fold and sew a tuck ⅜" (1.5 cm) deep (**drawing 4**). Fold the tuck over to the left; then fold the corners up to the center (**drawing 5**). Tack the corners to the base with a few hand stitches (**drawing 6**). Working from right to left in this manner, make one triangle after another, spacing them as shown (**drawing 7**); continue until the length of the pleated band equals T plus 3" (8 cm), which includes 1¾" (4 cm) at each end. Pleat the second band in the same way.

3. Attach the pleated trim

On each sleeve, center a pleated band along the top edge of the oversleeve; place the band ends at the underarm seam, evening out the space between the first and last triangles. Fold the ends of the strip under so they abut, and join with whipstitches. Sew the band on with an open backstitch, lifting the triangles as you go to make your work easier.

4. Embellish the oversleeves

About 2½" (6 cm) above each oversleeve hem, embroider over several of the printed flower motifs; use a doubled strand of tapestry wool, varying the colors as you wish. For each flower, make seven or eight long straight stitches that radiate from the center, like a star; then finish with a French knot at the center. You can adapt this idea to reflect the motifs on your particular fabric—use different embroidery stitches if you wish.

4.
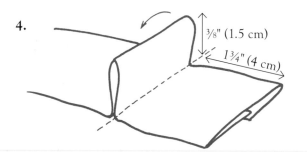
⅜" (1.5 cm)
1¾" (4 cm)

5.

6.
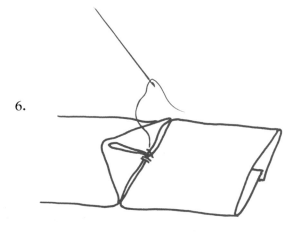

7.
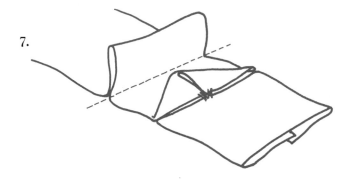

Gypsy chic

Refer to the basic techniques on pages 150–153

MATERIALS

+ Print fabric, 28" x 6" (70 x 15 cm): red on gray
+ Sewing thread: gray
+ Embroidery floss: silver
+ Polyester stuffing
+ Lightweight cardboard

SUPPLIES

+ Basic sewing supplies (see page 149)
+ Embroidery needle
+ Compass

Refer to the basic techniques on pages 150–153

From the closet
Lightweight woven-stripe cotton blouse with shirtfront yoke

1. Make the beads
Draw a circle about 1¼" (3 cm) in diameter on the cardboard. Cut it out for a template. Trace around it on the print fabric, marking about forty circles. Cut out the circles.

With your fingers, fold a narrow margin to the wrong side on one circle. With doubled thread, sew a small running stitch all around (**drawing 1**). Pull the thread so the edge starts to gather; tuck a small ball of stuffing into the pouch that forms. Pull the thread to close the pouch and secure the gathers with a few stitches (**drawing 2**). Make the rest of the beads.

2. Sew on the beads
Using doubled thread, sew the beads on one at a time. Arrange them along the edge of the shirtfront, spacing about ¾" (2 cm) apart. Stitch through the gathers on the bead back in a way that is secure but unobtrusive.

3. Cover the buttons
Remove the blouse buttons. Cover them with fabric in the same way you made the beads, but enlarge or reduce the template size if you need to.

Sew the buttons back onto the blouse. Stitch through the gathers on the back and try to create a shank so the button sits above the fabric when fastened.

4. Embroidery

Embroider two lines of French knots on the shirtfront, one on each side of the opening. Use two strands of floss and space the knots about ¼" (1 cm) apart along a fabric stripe.

1.

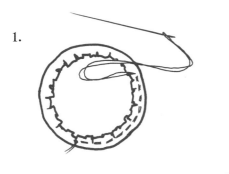

2.

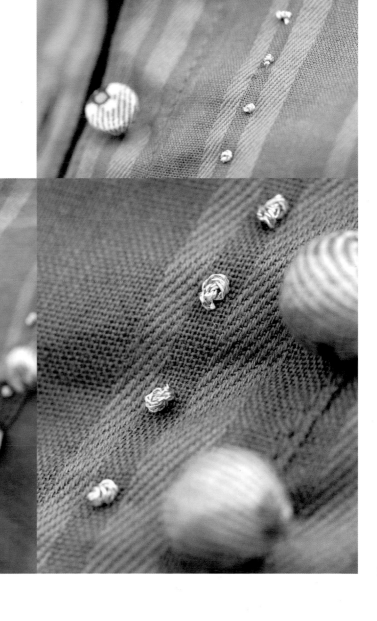

Folk cardigan

From the closet

Black cable crewneck pullover or sweater with long sleeves

Note

The length of the binding depends on the dimensions of your sweater. To determine, measure the length at center front and halfway around the neck, then add 2" (5 cm) for seams. If you can, choose a fabric at least this wide—for example, 36" (90 cm) so you don't have lots of seams in the binding.

1. Turn the pullover into a cardigan

Lay the sweater very flat, with the front up. Use pins to mark the center front from the bottom edge to the neckband (count the stitches between the cables to make sure you find the middle, so the halves will be symmetrical).

Carefully cut the front in two along the pins. Make sure your scissors are nice and sharp—and don't pierce the back.

Working with doubled black thread, immediately overcast the cut edges by hand so they don't ravel.

2. Create the binding

Mark two bands, each 1¾" (4.5 cm) high, all across the wrong side of the fabric. Cut them out. Lay each wrong-side up on your ironing board, and, pressing each fold with your iron as you go, turn up ¼" (1 cm) to the wrong side on both long edges and one end. Fold each band in half lengthwise, right-side-out, and press the fold.

MATERIALS

- Japanese print fabric, 44" x 12" (110 x 30 cm): multicolor on red
- Hook and eye closure
- Sewing thread: black, red
- Pearl cotton, size 5 or 8: red, dark pink, light pink

SUPPLIES

- Basic sewing supplies (see page 149)
- Sewing machine
- Embroidery needle

Refer to the basic techniques on pages 150–153

Tuck one center front edge of the sweater into the open edge of one of the bands; align the folded end of the band with the bottom edge of the sweater. Pin the band in place, making sure the knit edge is completely enclosed and stopping at the neck edge. Using doubled black thread and a whipstitch, sew the band to the right side of the sweater from the bottom to just below the neckband (**drawing 1**). Repeat on the inside of the sweater, then close the bottom of the band.

Mark the center back of the neckband with a pin inserted vertically. At the center front, fold the band at 45° to enclose the corner of the neckband; then pin the band in place just to the center back (**drawing 2**). Cut off the excess band, leaving an allowance to turn under. Working as before, sew the band to the neck, stopping short of the center back.

In the same way, fit and attach the other band to the other edge of the front opening and neckline. When you are sure the binding fits smoothly, turn the center back edges of the bands under so they abut, and finish stitching them in place.

1.

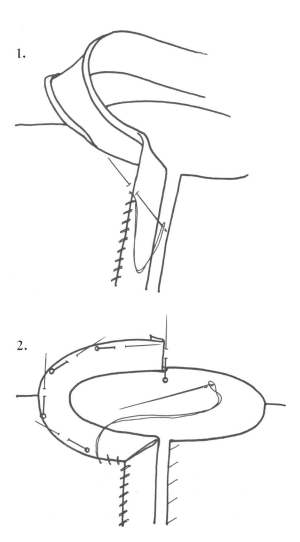

Folk cardigan continued

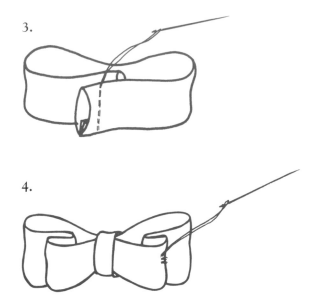

3.

4.

3. Make the bow

Cut two strips from the print fabric, one 14" x 5½" (35 x 14 cm) and one 2" x 1" (5 x 2.5 cm).

Fold the larger strip in half lengthwise, wrong-side out. Sew the long cut edges together with a ¼" (0.5 cm) seam allowance. Turn right-side-out; press. Fold the band in half crosswise and mark the middle of its length. Unfold, then form into a loop, slightly overlapping the ends at the marked midpoint. Using doubled red thread, baste through all layers across the midpoint (**drawing 3**). Pull the thread to gather the fabric as tightly as possible, then knot securely.

On both long edges of the smaller strip, fold and press ¼" (0.5 cm) to the wrong side. Wrap this piece, right-side-out, around the gathered middle of the first piece; overlap the ends and secure with several stitches.

On each half of the bow, tuck the end of the loop toward the center to create the illusion of a double loop; pin. Make sure the two halves are symmetrical as shown (**drawing 4**), and tack in place with a few stitches.

Sew the hook and eye closure to the inside of the cardigan, one piece on each side of the center at the neckline. Place the bow on the outside at the top of the right front. Sew in place with strong but unobtrusive stitches.

4. Embroidery

Use pearl cotton to embellish the cardigan fronts, working in a manner that suits the design of your sweater. For instance, outline some of the cables with an open backstitch, and sew long straight stitches over the popcorn bumps. Be spontaneous, and don't be afraid to mix the colors to make new shades.

shown on page 22

In the red

From the closet
Bright red brushed wool coat
with vertical pocket openings

Tips
• Don't hesitate to adjust the placement of the fabric trim to follow the seamlines of the coat you are using.
• Changing the shape of the collar is optional.

1. Embellish the collar
Reshape the points
Lay the collar very flat. Mark a new shape at the points, rounding the back edge slightly (**drawing 1**). Cut on the marked line. The measurement of the entire outside edge (including both ends) = L.

MATERIALS
+ Print fabric, 44" x 20" (110 x 50 cm): dark red and white on purple
+ Mother-of-pearl buttons, quantity and size to fit coat buttonholes
+ Sewing thread: red
+ Pearl cotton, size 5 or 8: red

SUPPLIES
+ Basic sewing supplies (see page 149)

Refer to the basic techniques on pages 150–153

1.

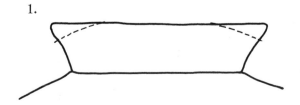

In the red continued

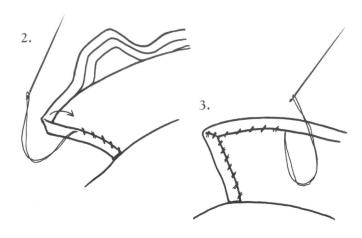

2.

3.

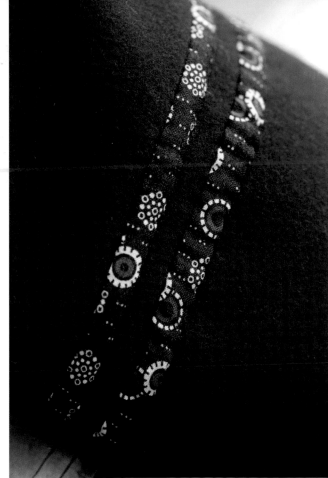

Trim

Mark a strip L x 1" (L x 2.5 cm) on the wrong side of the print fabric; mark another outline ¼" (0.5 cm) outside the first. Cut on the outside line. Lay the strip wrong-side-up on your ironing board, and, pressing each fold as you go, turn ¼" (0.5 cm) up on each edge. Pin the strip to the collar, wrapping it evenly over the edge and folding miters at the corners (**drawing 2**). Using a whipstitch, sew it first to the top of the collar, then to the underside (**drawing 3**).

Mark a strip L x ⅜" (L x 0.8 cm) on the wrong side of the print fabric. Working as for the first strip, add a narrow margin all around, cut out, and press the edges under. Pin this strip to the top side of the collar, parallel to the edges and a short space from the first strip. Turn the ends under, cutting off any excess. Whipstitch both edges to the collar.

2. Embellish the sleeves

Mark a line 3½" (9 cm) above the cuff all around each sleeve. The measurement around the sleeve on the line = T.

Mark four strips, each T x ⅜" (L x 0.8 cm) on the wrong side of the print fabric. Working as for the collar, add a narrow margin all around, cut out, and press the edges under. Pin one strip to a sleeve on the marked line; adjust the length if necessary. Whipstitch both edges to the sleeve. Apply a second band parallel to and a short space above the first one. Embellish the second sleeve in the same way.

3. Embellish the fronts

On each front, mark a vertical line along the pocket opening, extending it straight to the hemline. The length of this line plus 2" (5 cm) = Y. Mark another line parallel to this on the center-front side of the pocket welt, extending this line up to a "yoke" line and turning it toward the armhole. The length of this line plus 1¼" (3 cm) = Z (**drawing 4**).

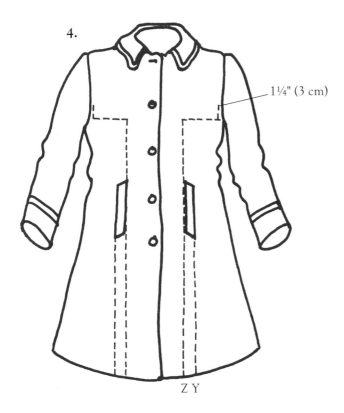

4.

1¼" (3 cm)

Z Y

Mark four strips on the wrong side of the fabric; make two of them Y x ⅜ (Y x 0.8 cm) and two Z x ⅜" (Z x 0.8 cm). Working as for the collar, add a narrow margin all around, cut out and press the edges under. Pin the strips to the marked lines (make the space between them the same as on the collar and sleeves); fold miters into the corners and turn the ends under as appropriate.

4. Make the flower trim

Cut eight strips from the fabric, each 1¼" x 8½" (3 x 21 cm). Press a narrow margin under on the long edges. Fold the strips in half lengthwise, right-side out, and press.

Twist each strip around on itself to form five loops crossing at a center point (**drawing 5**), and secure the shape with a few unobtrusive stitches in the center (**drawing 6**).

Sew a flower to the trim at the base of each sleeve, at the top of the pocket welt, at the turns by the "yoke" and at the armholes.

5. Don't forget the buttons!

Remove the original buttons. Use pearl cotton to sew on the new buttons.

5.

6.

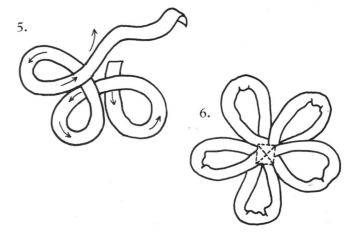

43

JET SET

Free spirit
Summer white, anyone?
With a fragile flower on
one strap and delicate
tulle appliqués dotted
with embroidery,
this tank top promises
sweet times to come!
Instructions p. 60

Disco tunic

Bright sequins that cover the collar band and large paillettes that dance with your every movement play up the bubbly, stylized print on this tee. No polka dots? No worries, you can add effervescence to a plain tee, too. *Instructions p. 62*

Marco polo

Voilà: the black polo shirt reimagined. Replace the placket and lighten up the somber color with a sequin-trimmed ivory sash that ties in a sexy bow in back. Alluring—without a doubt! *Instructions p. 64*

Vagabond

Once a simple sundress, now an outfit with plenty of self-esteem: Disguise the button band, play up the neckline and hem with bands of contrast fabric, and add bows (definitely not for the shy).
The world awaits!
Instructions p. 66

50

Bead bazaar
This svelte top makes you the envy of *tout le monde*. Sparkling beads, pearl buttons, classy red piping—what more could you ask for when you want to be ultrafeminine and just a touch *girly*!
Instructions p. 68

Flower festival
You'll adore brightening
up your wintry clothes.
It's so simple: scatter
sequins like little posies
along the neck and waist,
and trim one shoulder
with a fabulous lace
blossom. Totally chic.
Instructions p. 70

55

Hong Kong girl

Here's a serious makeover for a long dress with short sleeves. Turn the skirt into long sleeves, add contrast trim at the neck and waist, and burnish the fabric with gold paint. It's now a smart little tunic with lots of Asian style—perfect for a special evening.

Instructions p. 72

Duty-free skirt
Get ready for take-off:
Simply embroider the
outline of a jet plane
on a denim miniskirt—
front and back. Travel
won't be dull!
Instructions p. 76

Free spirit

From the closet
White tank top with thin straps, gathered at the center-front neckline

Tip
To keep the top svelte, always knot and cut the embroidery floss when moving from one spot to another.

1. Apply the motifs
Prep the pieces
Make two photocopies of the blue and yellow templates on page 158, enlarging to 200%. From one copy, cut out the blue motifs; from the other copy, cut out the yellow motifs. Make a photocopy of the flowers at the bottom of the page at 100% and cut out the motifs.

Pin each of the cut-out templates to the stretch tulle. Trace the outlines, remove the templates and cut out the motifs.

Apply the background motifs
Arranging them as shown on page 158, pin the two tulle shapes cut from the blue templates onto the front of the tank top. Sew them on, using a short running stitch close to the edge, in various colors of pearl cotton (**drawing 1**). Referring to the photos, outline some of the interior areas and fill them with lines of runnng stitches.

Apply the top motifs
Superimpose the tulle pieces you cut from the yellow templates onto the background motifs. To attach them, sew a running

MATERIALS
• Stretch tulle, 20" x 20"
(50 x 50 cm): white
• Pearl cotton, size 5 or 8:
marine blue, sky blue, orange,
yellow, chocolate
• Embroidery floss: silver

SUPPLIES
• Basic sewing supplies
(see page 149)
• Embroidery needle

**Refer to the basic
techniques on pages
150–153**

stitch up the center of each shape (or lobe where the shape is complex) with silver embroidery floss; leave the edges of these motifs loose, as shown (**drawing 2**).

2. Flowers add lots of charm
Stack the four flower cutouts from largest on the bottom to smallest on top. Place them on the tank at the base of one strap and secure with several silver-floss stitches in the center.

1.

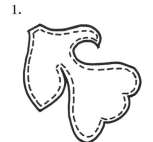

2.

Disco tunic

From the closet

From the closet
Long, fluid, scoop-neck jersey T-shirt, white with polka dots, with a 1¼" (3 cm)-wide neckband

1. Embellish the neckband
Referring to the photos, completely cover the neckband with parallel rows of sequins. Make each row a single color and use pearl cotton to sew. Arrange them like scales, overlapping each sequin on the previous one and attaching them with a backstitch. Knot and cut the thread only when you need to refill the needle (**drawings 1 and 2**).

2. Add paillettes to the front
Decorate the front of the T-shirt with paillettes. Sew them on one by one, knotting and cutting the thread on the inside for each. Place some of the paillettes along the bottom row of sequins so as to blend the two embellished areas, and then scatter the others below the band with diminishing density toward the bust. Place one color at a time so you can balance their impact.

MATERIALS
+ Metallic sequins, size 0.5 cm (center hole): midnight blue, turquoise, silver, red, fuchsia
+ Paillettes, size 2.5 cm (off-center hole): 4 yellow, 4 pink, 4 orange, 3 lime green, 3 metallic green
+ Pearl cotton, size 5 or 8: white

SUPPLIES
+ Basic sewing supplies (see page 149)
+ Embroidery needle

Refer to the basic techniques on pages 150–153

1.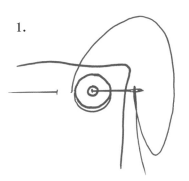

2.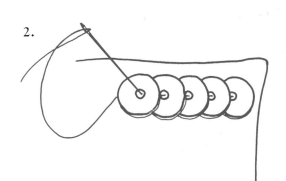

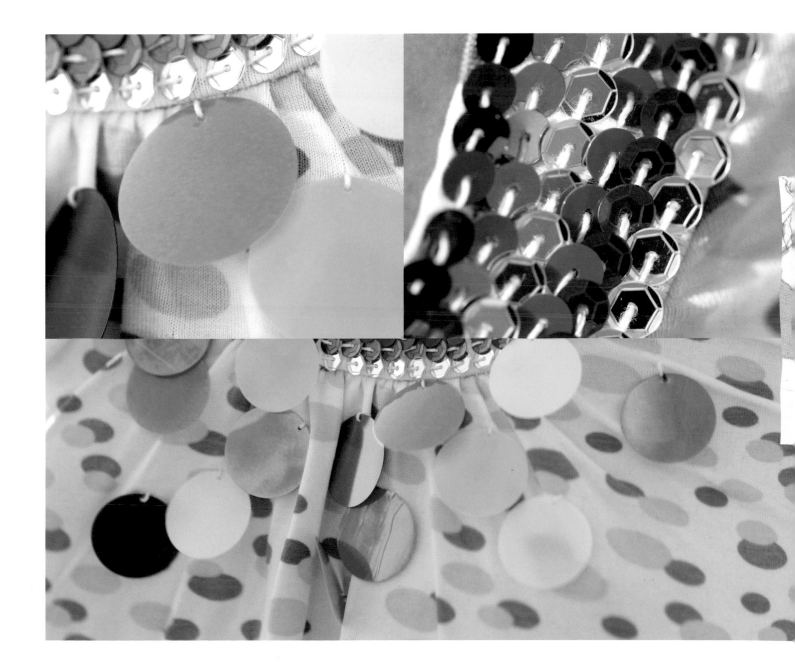

Marco polo

From the closet

Short-sleeve black polo shirt with button cuffs and satin placket facings

1. Cover up the buttonholes

Remove the buttons. Measure the length and width of the buttonhole band. Mark a strip this size on the wrong side of the satin fabric; mark another outline ¼" (0.5 cm) outside the first. Cut on the outside line. Lay the strip wrong-side up on your ironing board, and, pressing the folds as you go, turn ¼" (0.5 cm) up on each edge. Pin the strip right-side-up over the buttonhole band; make sure it lies smoothly. Sew all four edges in place with small whipstitches.

2. Add a classy accent

Using black pearl cotton, sew a line of iridescent black sequins along each shoulder seam.

3. Create the sash

Make the main piece

Your waist measurement plus 1" (2.5 cm) = T. On the wrong side of the ivory print fabric, mark a rectangle T x 8" (T x 20 cm); mark another outline ½" (1 cm) outside the first. Cut on the outside line. Fold the rectangle in half lengthwise, wrong-side out. Leaving a ½" (1 cm) seam allowance and leaving a 4" (10 cm) opening in the middle of the long side, sew the open edges closed. Trim the seam allowance at each corner. Turn the band right-side out. Fold the seam allowance in at the

MATERIALS

+ Satin fabric, 12" x 4"
(30 x 10 cm): black
+ Print fabric, tiny black circles
on ivory: 36" x 20" (90 x 50 cm)
+ Sequins, size 0.5 cm (center
hole): iridescent black, red, pink,
fluorescent yellow, blue, gold
+ Sequins, size 1 cm (off-center
hole), translucent blue
+ Snap, size 2 cm
+ Sewing thread: white, black
+ Pearl cotton, size 5 or 8: black

SUPPLIES

+ Basic sewing supplies
(see page 149)
+ Sewing machine
+ Embroidery needle

Refer to the basic techniques on pages 150–153

64

opening, press and whipstitch closed. Using black pearl cotton, sew seeding stitches along both long edges, incorporating sequins of both sizes and all colors at random as shown in the photos.

Using a doubled length of thread in a hand-sewing needle and leaving a long tail at the beginning, sew running stitches along one end of the band; without cutting the thread, turn and sew a second line of running stitches parallel to the first and a short distance away. Pull the thread ends to gather the band as tightly as possible; tie off. Gather the other end in the same way. Sew the snap to the band ends (so the ends overlap).

Make a faux bow
Mark three rectangles, each 8" x 5½" (20 x 14 cm), on the wrong side of the ivory fabric. Working as for the main piece, add a ½" (1 cm) margin all around and cut out. Fold, sew and turn each piece the same way you made the main piece.

Fold each piece in half crosswise to find its midpoint. Using doubled thread in a hand-sewing needle, sew running stitches across the middle of each, from one long edge to the other. Gather the fabric as tightly as possible and secure the thread. Fold each piece along the gathers.

Stack pieces, aligning the gathered folds. Sew them together with an overcast stitch, being sure to go through all layers. Sew the bow to the top of the overlap end of the main piece.

Add the sash to the shirt
Lay the polo shirt flat. Mark each side seam with a pin 5" (12 cm) below the armhole. Mark the center front at the same level with another pin. Fold the sash in half crosswise to find the midpoint; place the midpoint of the top edge on the center-front pin. Smooth the sash out to align the top edge with the pin at each side seam and pin in place. Using pearl cotton, attach the sash to the polo shirt at each side seam with a swing tack (page 151). Begin and end the swing tack on the side seam about ¾" (2 cm) above the top of the sash and make the bar about ¾" (2 cm) long. Be sure to end the thread securely on the inside of the shirt (**drawing below**).

Vagabond

From the closet

Red cotton-and-linen sheath sundress with skinny straps and a button placket, mid-thigh length

1. Simplify the closure

Remove the buttons. Measure the length and width of the buttonhole band. Mark a strip this size on the wrong side of the red fabric; mark another outline ¼" (0.5 cm) outside the first. Cut on the outside line. Lay the strip wrong-side up on your ironing board, and, pressing the folds as you go, turn ¼" (0.5 cm) up on each edge. Pin the strip right-side up over the buttonhole band; make sure it lies smoothly. Sew all four edges in place with small whipstitches. Sew the snaps to the inside of the placket.

2. Dress up the hemline

If your dress does not have side slits at the hem, remove the stitches from the bottom 4" (10 cm) of each side seam and hem each edge with small invisible stitches.

Using doubled thread, sew running stitches along the front hem, close to the edge. Pull the thread to gather the fabric until the lower edge measures 15" (38 cm) from slit to slit; tie off securely. Gather the back hem in the same way.

Mark two rectangles, each 16" x 3" (40 x 7 cm), on the wrong side of each fabric. Cut them out. With the right sides together, place each floral band on a red band. Leaving a ½" (1 cm) seam allowance, sew both ends and one long side. Trim the seam allowance at the sewn corners and turn the bands right-side out. Fold ½" (1 cm) to the inside on each open edge,

MATERIALS

+ Red fabric: 44" x 6" (110 x 15 cm)
+ Sheer floral-print fabric: 44" x 6" (110 x 15 cm)
+ Stretch tulle, blue: 30" x 4" (80 x 10 cm)
+ Sewing thread: to match fabrics
+ 4 snaps, size 1.4 cm (or larger)

SUPPLIES

+ Basic sewing supplies (see page 149)
+ Sewing machine

Refer to the basic techniques on pages 150–153

and press the folds with an iron. Insert the front hem of the dress into the open edge of one of the bands (floral fabric facing out as shown), overlapping slightly. Pin. Sew the floral side of the band to the outside of the dress with whipstitches, then sew the red side to the inside of the dress. Attach the other band to the back hem in the same way.

3. Add a collar

Mark the midpoint of the back neckline with a pin. The measurement from the pin to the placket (along the top of the underarm) plus ½" (2 cm) = L.

Cut two rectangles, each L x 3" (L x 7 cm), from each fabric. With the right sides together, place each floral band on a red band. Leaving a ½" (1 cm) seam allowance and leaving a small opening for turning on one long edge, sew around all four edges. Trim the seam allowance at the corners and turn the collars right-side out. Fold the seam allowances in at the openings and whipstitch closed.

With the outside of the dress facing you, position one collar along the neckline between the center back and placket, orienting it so it extends up, with the floral side against the strap; pin to the top edge of the dress. Whipstitch the dress and collar edges together and then fold the collar down. Attach the other collar to the other half of the dress in the same way.

4. Stylish finish: two small bows

Cut two strips, each 32" x 2" (80 x 5 cm), from the tulle. Fold each in half lengthwise, then complete as for the collars (don't sew along the fold). Tie a bow with each strip and sew one to the dress front at the base of each strap.

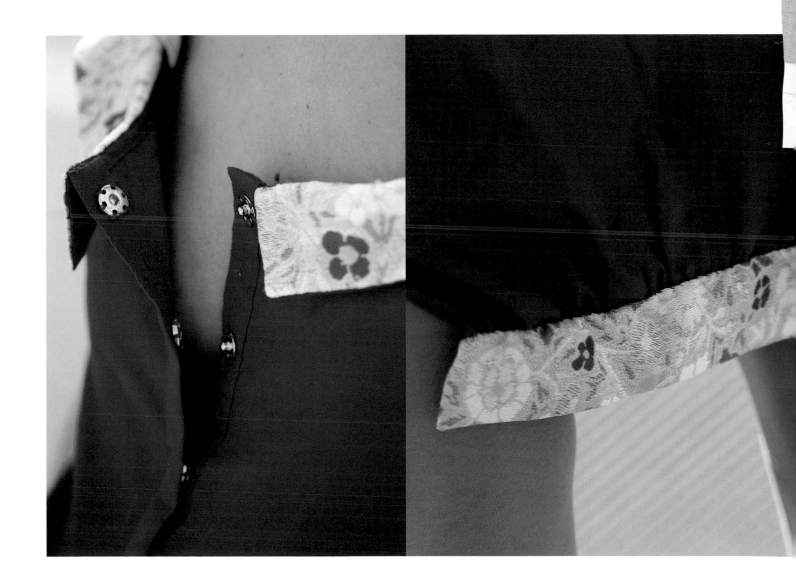

Bead bazaar

From the closet
Tightly knit black angora pullover with round neck and long, short, or no sleeves

Note
The piping adds stability to the neck and armhole edges, but if it's too tight, the edges will bind. While you pin it on, be sure to keep the garment edges slightly stretched.

1. First, make the neckline sexy!
Photocopy the template on page 157, enlarging to 150%, and cut it out.

Lay the sweater flat with the front up; slide the cardboard inside and smooth the neck and bust area over it. Pin the pattern to it, placing the neck-edge corner of the strap on the shoulder seam. Baste along the neck and armhole edges of the pattern. Unpin the pattern and flip it over, then repeat this process to mark the other half of the front. If necessary, extend the basting across the center front and to the side seams. Turn the sweater over and mark the armholes (but not the neckline) on the back in the same way.

Set your sewing machine to a medium zigzag stitch. Sew close to the basted outlines (for the back neck, sew just below the ribbing or neckband); stretch the knit ever so slightly as you go. Go around each outline twice. Remove the basting.

Cut the neckline and armholes out just outside the zigzag stitching.

MATERIALS
+ Piping, 3 yards (250 cm): rose and white stripe
+ 45 small mother-of pearl buttons
+ Assorted matte and shiny beads: various colors, shapes and sizes
+ Sewing thread: black
+ Cardboard: size to fit inside sweater

SUPPLIES
+ Basic sewing supplies (see page 149)
+ Sewing machine

Refer to the basic techniques on pages 150–153

2. Add the piping

At the neck and each armhole, turn the zigzag edge to the inside of the sweater and whipstitch it in place.

Starting and ending at the side seam, pin the piping around one armhole (be sure the flange is on the inside of the garment). Fold the piping ends down along the side seam and cut off the excess. Repeat for the other armhole. Pin piping to the neck in the same way, but start and stop at the center back. Sew the piping on by hand using small whipstitches; pass through only the top layer of the knit and catch the piping right below the cord (**drawing 1**). With the inside of the garment facing you, whipstitch the piping ends together as shown (**drawing 2**).

3. Embellish the edges

Using doubled thread, sew the beads to the neck and armhole edges. As shown in the photos, you can apply the beads in a random pattern, singly or in groups, but be sure to stitch through the knit fabric only, not through the piping. Finish embellishing by sewing the pearl buttons on at irregular intervals.

1.

2.

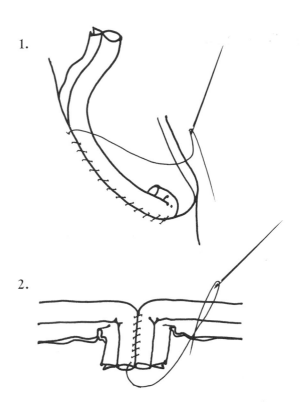

Flower festival

From the closet
Blue-gray wrap-front top with four-button closure at the waist

1. Add sequin flowers

Plan the placement for the sequin flowers on the overlap half of the top. Take your inspiration from the photos: place a grouping at the waist, another less important grouping at the shoulder, and scattered single blossoms in between. Place a chalk mark or pin where you want the center of each blossom to be. Refer to the instructions below to make the flowers; use two strands of embroidery floss and knot and cut the thread after making each one. Experiment to get the hang of it!

Four-petal flower
Bring the needle from back to front at the mark. Slide one of the smallest (size 0.4 cm) sequins over the needle and sew it on with a single stitch; sew on three more sequins, arranging in a diamond shape.

Eight- or twelve-petal flower
Use the medium-size sequins (size 0.6 cm). To begin, make a loosely spaced four-petal flower, then top it with one or two more, offsetting the sequins on each layer and centering each closer to the middle of the first flower.

Full-blown flower
Use the large sequins with the off-center hole. Sew on lots, first arranging in a ring and then filling in with more until the center is full and floppy.

MATERIALS

+ Scallop-edge 6" (16 cm)-wide lace trim, pink-and-yellow: 1 yard (90 cm)
+ Sequins, size 0.4 cm (center hole): iris red
+ Sequins, size 0.6 cm (center hole): matte bright red, iris black
+ Transparent sequins, size 1 cm (off-center hole): yellow, blue
+ Sewing thread: yellow
+ Embroidery floss: blue
+ Safety pin

SUPPLIES

+ Basic sewing supplies (see page 149)
+ Sewing machine
+ Embroidery needle

Refer to the basic techniques on pages 150–153

2. Create the lace flower brooch

Cut a 25" (62 cm)-long piece from the lace. On the long straight edge, fold ¼" (0.5 cm) over to the wrong side twice; baste. Do the same at each end. With the sewing machine, sew through all layers close to the first fold.

Now, along the long hemmed edge, make a 1½" (4 cm)-deep accordion fold onto the right side of the lace (**drawing at right**). Using doubled sewing thread in a hand-sewing needle, sew long running stitches through all layers along the bottom edge as shown. Pull the thread to gather the lace as tightly as possible; secure, but don't cut the thread. Arrange the gathered lace into a flower and stitch together on the back.

From the remaining lace, cut three narrow strips ranging from 4" to 12" (10 to 30 cm) in length. Sew one end of each to the back of the flower. Safety-pin the flower near the shoulder on the embellished side of the top.

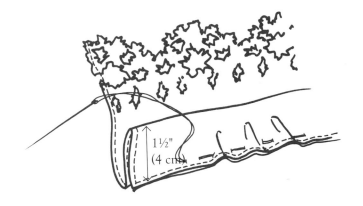

71

Hong Kong girl

From the closet

Knee-length jersey dress in a large-scale-floral print, with short sleeves and V-neck extending to a waistline seam

Tip

It's important to maintain the elasticity of the jersey while you reattach the skirt. To do this, you can slip the dress over the back of a chair, or cut a piece of cardboard to half your bust circumference and slide it inside the dress.

1. Radical surgery!

Take out the stitches that hold the neckband to the dress at the point of the V and separate the ends of the band.

Lay the dress flat. Draw a horizontal line across it 1½" (4 cm) below the point of the V; draw a second line ½" (1 cm) below the first. Cut through both layers at once on the lower line.

On the tube that was just cut off the dress, draw a line 14" (36 cm) above the hem; cut on this line. On the top portion, cut off the vertical seams. You now have two rectangles and one tube.

2. Paint some of the motifs

Slide the plastic bag inside the hemmed jersey tube. Apply gold paint to the flower motifs on about 8" (20 cm) of the fabric below the top edge. Let the paint dry, then turn the tube over and paint the other side. Also paint the motifs along the top 8" (20 cm) of each flat piece. Let the paint dry and fix it according to the manufacturer's instructions.

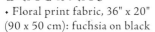

MATERIALS

+ Floral print fabric, 36" x 20" (90 x 50 cm): fuchsia on black
+ Sequins, assorted sizes: fuchsia, yellow, red, translucent pink, iridescent clear
+ Sewing thread: black, pink
+ Round elastic, 1 yard (100 cm)
+ Plastic bag (to protect garment during painting)
+ Cardboard: about 10" x 4" (25 x 10 cm)

SUPPLIES

+ Basic sewing supplies (see page 149)
+ Sewing machine
+ Safety pin
+ Artist's paintbrush
+ Fabric paint in gold

Refer to the basic techniques on pages 150–153

3. Cover the neckband

Mark the center back of the neckband with a pin. The measurement should be from the pin to the point of the V, plus ½" (1 cm) = L.

Mark two strips, each L x 2½" (L x 6 cm), on the wrong side of the black fabric. Cut them out. Lay each wrong-side up on your ironing board and, pressing the folds with the iron as you go, turn up ½" (0.5 cm) on all edges.

Starting at the center back, lay each strip right-side up on the neck band; at the center front, tuck the ends under the waist seam. Pin in place (if the fabric strip is wider than your neckband, wrap the excess to the inside). Whipstitch the new band to the old along all edges. At the center front, overlap the ends and tuck them under the waist seam; stitch all layers.

4. Reattach the skirt...

Fold ¾" (1.5 cm) to the inside all along the top of the hemmed tube. Baste, then sew by machine ½" (1 cm) from the edge, leaving a 1" (2.5 cm) opening. Thread the elastic through this casing with the aid of the safety pin. Pull the elastic ends until the top of the tube measures the same as the lower edge of the dress top. Tie the elastic ends together, feed them into the casing and sew the opening closed.

With both pieces right-side out, slide the tube over the dress, placing the gathered edge on the marked line and aligning the side seams. Sew together by hand using open backstitches.

Hong Kong girl *continued*

5. ...and turn the flat pieces into long sleeves

Make the sleeves

Following **drawings 1** and **2** below, mark two small trapezoids on the wrong side of the black fabric and one large trapezoid on the wrong side of each remaining piece of jersey. Mark a second outline ¼" (1 cm) outside the first and cut the pieces on the outer line. Lay the jersey pieces wrong-side up. Place a black piece right-side down on each, aligning the side and bottom (18" [45 cm]) edges. Pin and sew each set ¼" (1 cm) from the bottom edge. Fold the black fabric over, on the seam, to the right side of the jersey; press the fold. Fold under ¼" (1 cm) along the top edge of the black fabric; pin and then whipstitch to the jersey.

Fold each sleeve in half lengthwise, aligning the angled edges. Sew each along the angled edge, ¼" (1 cm) from the edge.

Attach the sleeves

Measure around the hem on one of the short sleeves. This measurement = T. Mark the midpoint of the top edge of each long sleeve with a pin. Using doubled thread, sew long running stitches along the top of each long sleeve, about ¼" (0.5 cm) from the edge, then pull the thread to gather the edge so it measures T; knot the thread.

Turn the dress inside-out. Cut the cardboard so its width is equal to half of T. From the hem, slide the cardboard inside one of the short sleeves (**drawing 3**). Slide one of the long sleeves, wrong-side out, over the cardboard so that it overlaps the cuff by ¼" (0.5 cm); align the underarm seams and place the pin at the fold (middle) of the cuff. Pin the top of the long sleeve to the cuff and then sew together using open backstitch (**drawing 4**). Repeat to assemble the other sleeve. Turn the dress right-side-out. Slide the cardboard into the cuff of one of the sleeves again. Sew the bottom of the cuff to the long sleeve with invisible stitches. Repeat to complete the other sleeve.

1.

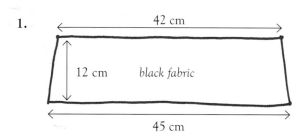

42 cm

12 cm   *black fabric*

45 cm

2.

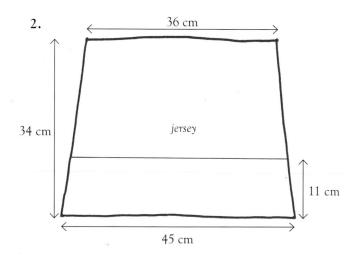

36 cm

34 cm   *jersey*

11 cm

45 cm

3.

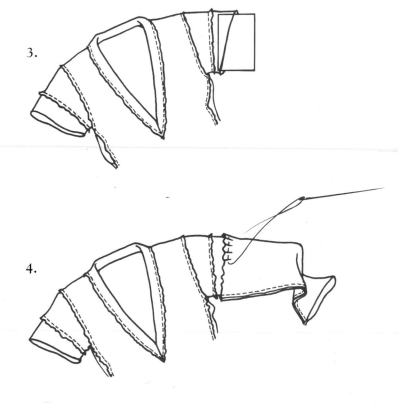

4.

6. Add a sash with long tails

Make the sash

Mark three strips, each 25" x 4" (62 x 10 cm), on the wrong side of the black fabric. Cut them out. With the right sides together, sew them together end-to-end to make one long strip. Fold this in half lengthwise, wrong-side out. Sew along one end and the long open edge, ¼" (0.5 cm) from the edge. Turn the sash right-side out and tuck in ¼" (0.5 cm) at the open end; whipstitch closed. Fold the sash in half crosswise to find the midpoint. Lay the sash across the dress, placing the midpoint of the upper edge just below the point of the V. Attach the top of the sash with several small stitches across the area below the V.

Belt loops

From the remaining jersey scraps, cut two rectangles, each 2" x ¾" (5 x 2 cm). On all four edges of each, fold ¼" (0.5 cm) to the wrong side and secure with invisible stitches. Mark the center back of the dress on the waist seam. Place the belt loops vertically over the seam, each about 2" (5 cm) from the center back. Sew the ends of the belt loops securely to the dress. Feed the sash through the loops (tie after putting on the dress).

7. Finish with sequin accents

Sew a sprinkling of sequins over each painted flower. Use doubled pink thread and affix each with a single long straight stitch; because the paint has made the jersey stiff, you can carry the thread from sequin to sequin on the wrong side instead of knotting and cutting it after sewing each one on.

JET SET

Duty-free skirt

From the closet
Denim skirt, above-knee length

Tip
You can choose a different motif, of course; the essential thing is that it be scaled to fit on your skirt. If you want to work from a photograph, trace the key lines and details first and adapt them to read well in two dimensions. Then photocopy the tracing, enlarging to the desired size.

1. Prep the motif
Photocopy the template on page 159. Lay the skirt flat. Place the dressmaker's carbon ink-side-down on the area you want to embroider. Place the photocopy on the carbon paper; pin both papers to the cloth. Trace the lines of the design with a stylus or the tip of a knitting needle. Remove the papers. If the design isn't as clear as you'd like, use dressmaker's white chalk to supplement the tracing.

2. Embroider the design
Using the photos as inspiration, embroider the design in various colors of pearl cotton. As shown with the template on page 159, work the main outlines in stem stitch, the letters in closed backstitch, and the radiating lines and short dash lines in long straight stitch.

MATERIALS
+ Pearl cotton, size 5 or 8: black, tan, soft gray, orange, turquoise, sky blue, white, golden yellow
+ Dressmaker's white carbon paper

SUPPLIES
+ Basic sewing supplies (see page 149)
+ Embroidery needle

Refer to the basic techniques on pages 150–153

Tee time top
It's all a matter of
buttons! Instead
of letting your stash
languish in a box
at the bottom of a
drawer, show them off
this way, sewn all over
the sleeves of a tee—
it's just the ticket.
Instructions p. 94

79

"Petal" pushers

Break time: Whether it's mid-term or just the weekend, don't wait to jump into cute cropped jeans. Make fun appliqués with your computer and transfer paper. Pair with a twin set and ballet flats.
Instructions p. 96

Very vintage
A round collar covered in a sweet floral and finished with a little pleated ruffle, buttons covered with the same floral, sleeves trimmed to match and decorated with a small velvet bow, delicate embroidery... perfect to the last detail!
Instructions p. 98

82

Twist skirt

Here's a skirt just meant for greeting sunny days. Dress it up with appliqué triangles cut from a contrasting print and embellished with a touch of paint. A petite frill of red tulle makes twirling irresistible!
Instructions p. 100

Montmartre tank

This tank top is so simple: all you do is add three cloth straps, each in a different print, securing the ends under playful buttons. Totally discreet; charmingly rogue! *Instructions p. 102*

87

Coed blouse
Get the ingénue look by restyling a classic blouse: remove the collar, give the neckline a gracious curve and add a big covered button. Create a yoke by adding a soft ruffle, then fill it in with pearl beads and buttons—it's sixties chic!
Instructions p. 104

Bead it!

An everyday skirt customized to light up the night. What's the secret? Paint shimmery motifs in pearlized blue and embellish them with sparkling bronze-color beads. Then make a black silk sash to drape and tie seductively around the hips.
Instructions p. 108

91

Latin Quarter tunic

Go for *trompe l'œil* on a classic
crewneck pullover! Cut off
the long sleeves and hide
what's left under puffs sewn
from a cute cotton print. To
create faux pockets, add
appliquéd welts above
embroidered edges. Complete
the effect with covered buttons.
Instructions p. 110

TEE TIME TOP

MATERIALS

+ Narrow trim for neckline and cuffs if your top is plain: gold
+ Small shank buttons, number and size to match garment buttonholes: black
+ An assortment of mother-of-pearl and glass buttons, up to ¾" (1.7 cm) in diameter: black
+ 10 each engraved metal buttons and dangle trinkets: antique finish
+ Embroidery floss: gold
+ Sewing thread: black, gold to match the trim if adding

SUPPLIES

+ Basic sewing supplies (see page 149)
+ Seam ripper
+ Embroidery needle
+ Sewing machine (for applying the trim)

Refer to the basic techniques on pages 150–153

 GARMENT TO START WITH
Pullover knit top with short, cuffed sleeves, V-neck and long button placket, with or without narrow gold trim along the neckline and cuffs

Tips

• You can sometimes find full cards of old buttons at thrift shops and flea markets. Keep an eye out as well for inexpensive, secondhand clothes: even if they're not wearable, they may be worth buying for their buttons!
• To protect the finish on your various buttons, always turn the garment inside-out when you launder it.

1. Add the trim

If your top doesn't have trim around the neck and cuffs, add it. First, carefully remove the buttons. Pin or baste the trim in place, taking care not to pull it tighter than the cuff or neckband and turning the ends under neatly. If the trim is too thick to turn under, cut it to the exact length needed and overcast or zigzag the ends so they don't ravel.

Using thread to match the trim, sew the trim on by machine from the right side, Depending on your trim, you can probably just attach each edge with a medium-to-long zigzag stitch (a small stitch will stiffen the work).

2. Every detail counts: change the buttons!

If you haven't yet done so, carefully remove the original buttons. Replace them with the new shank buttons.

3. Embellish the sleeves

Divide the assorted buttons and the charms into two groups of equal impact. Sew them randomly to the sleeves as shown, using embroidery floss and knotting and cutting the thread after attaching each one.

"PETAL" PUSHERS

FROM THE CLOSET
Denim jeans, cropped or full-length

Tip
To find pretty floral motifs suitable for transfer embellishments, look in wallpaper catalogs, search out interesting fabrics, look at botanical reference books, etc.

1. Prep for a trendy length
If you want to shorten your jeans, try them on and, with a pin, mark the desired length on one leg. Take jeans off, lay them flat and draw a line 2½" (6 cm) below the pin, parallel to the hem. Draw across the other leg at the same distance above the hem. Cut each leg on the marked line.

2. Cuff the legs
By hand, secure the cut edge of each leg with small overcast stitches. Pressing each fold with the iron as you go, turn 1¼" (3 cm) up twice to the outside. Secure the top edge of the cuff to the leg with invisible stitches.

Cut the velvet ribbon into two equal lengths; trim the ends at an angle. Tie each length into a bow. Sew a bow to the cuff on each leg, centering it over the side seam and attaching through the back of the knot.

MATERIALS
- Velvet ¾" (2 cm)-wide ribbon, 24" (60 cm): light pink
- Sewing thread: pink
- Pearl cotton, size 5 or 8: dark pink, light pink, tan
- Transfer paper (for desktop printer)

SUPPLIES
- Basic sewing supplies (see page 149)
- Embroidery needle
- Computer, scanner, color printer

Refer to the basic techniques on pages 150–153

3. Add floral embellishments

Select a floral motif from a magazine, book or other source. Scan it. Print the motif onto the transfer paper; use pink and sepia tints and, referring to the photos, create two sizes—one to fit on a back pocket and one larger. Cut out each motif along its edges.

Following the paper manufacturer's instructions, tranfer the motifs to your jeans. Place the motifs as shown.

Draw a few natural-looking stems and leaves freehand around the motifs. Embroider these using closed backstitch and tan pearl cotton. On each of the motifs, embroider some leaf veins in the same way or with long straight stitches. Then, using the dark pink and light pink pearl cotton, outline some of the petals and add some veins to them. Work some French knots in the flower centers. Make sure you don't sew the pockets closed when you embroider! (You can slide a piece of cardboard inside to make sure you stitch through only one layer.)

VERY VINTAGE

FROM THE CLOSET
Short-sleeved, pale yellow dotted-swiss blouse with V-neck and a small or band collar

Tips
• To neatly fold the edges over on the collar pieces, first baste around each close to the edge. Make a cardboard template of the pattern and center it on a collar piece. Pull the basting thread up to tightly wrap the fabric over the template edges. Press with an iron, then remove the basting and template.
• If the sleeves of your blouse do not finish with a ruffle, use running stitch to sew round elastic about 1¼" (3 cm) above the hem of each; tie off to fit loosely at your biceps.

1. Add a collar
To make the collar, measure the base of the blouse collar (along the seam, from one front edge around the neck to the other front edge). Half of this length = L.

Photocopy the template on page 154. Shorten or lengthen it so that the long straight edge = L. Cut it out.

Fold the print fabric in half crosswise, wrong-side out. Position the template on it, aligning the dotted line with the fold. Draw around template; then draw another outline ⅜" (1 cm) outside the first. Cut fabric piece out on the outer line; then cut another identical piece. Also cut a collar from batting, but don't add the margin.

Unfold each fabric collar piece, lay them wrong-side up on your ironing board, and, pressing as you go, fold up ⅜" (1 cm) all around each.

MATERIALS
• Floral print fabric, 24" x 12" (60 x 30 cm): faded rose on yellow
• Batting : 24" x 4" (60 x 10 cm)
• Sewing thread: yellow
• Satin ⅝" (1.5 cm)-wide pleated ribbon, 60" (150 cm): pink
• Velvet ½" (1.3 cm)-wide ribbon, 8" (20 cm): light pink
• Darning thread: three shades of pink, light green, mustard yellow
• Lightweight cardboard

SUPPLIES
• Basic sewing supplies (see page 149)
• Embroidery needle
• Compass

Refer to the basic techniques on pages 150–153

Lay one collar wrong-side up. Pin the tight edge of the pleated ribbon around the rounded edge, on the folded-over margin. Sew on with running stitch (**drawing 1**).

Slide the batting under the margins of the other collar piece. Place the ruffled collar right-side up on top of this, aligning the edges. Baste together all around, then, with small running stitches, sew the rounded edges together through all layers.

Attach and embellish
Remove the basting from its neck edge and slide the new collar onto the one on the blouse, aligning the open edge with the seam. Whipstitch it in place, first on the inside of the blouse, then on the outside.

To give definition to the flower print, sew around some of the motifs with small running stitches through all layers.

2. Embellish the sleeves

The distance around each sleeve at the top of the ruffle (or elastic) = T. Cut two pieces of pleated ribbon, each T + ¾" (T + 2 cm) long. Pin the tight edge of each around a sleeve, above the gathering; fold under the ends at the underarm seam. Sew in place with running stitches.

On the wrong side of the floral fabric, mark two strips, each T x ⅝" (T x 1.5 cm). Mark an outline ⅜" (1 cm) outside the first; cut out the strips on the outer line. Lay them wrong-side up on your ironing board, and, pressing each fold with the iron as you go, turn up ⅜" (1 cm) on each edge. Pin each strip over the pleated ribbon on a sleeve, positioning so the ribbon peeks out below it, and sew the top edge in place.

For each bow, cut one piece of velvet ribbon 3" (7 cm) long and one piece 1¼" (3 cm) long. Fold each longer piece into a loop and sew the ends together with a few stitches (**drawing 2**). Wrap a short piece around this; sew as shown (**drawing 3**). Sew a bow to the fabric band on each sleeve, opposite the underarm seam.

3. Cover the buttons

Remove the buttons from the blouse. On the cardboard, draw a circle with a diameter twice that of one of the buttons and cut it out for a template. Draw around it on the print fabric, marking a circle for each button. Cut out the circles.

With your fingers, fold a narrow margin to the wrong side on one circle. With doubled thread, sew a small running stitch all around. Pull the thread so the edge starts to gather; tuck a button into the pouch that forms. Pull the thread to close the pouch; secure the gathers with a few stitches. Repeat to cover the rest of the buttons. Sew the buttons back onto the blouse, attaching each through the gathers on the backs.

4. Embroidery

Embroider small flowers at regular intervals among the dots on the blouse fabric (**drawing 4**). Create them one at a time, knotting and cutting the thread on the wrong side after each. For the petals, use all three pink threads together: Make one upright lazy daisy stitch, and then, on each side of its base, a long straight stitch. To fill its center, make two vertical long straight stitches with mustard yellow. To make a stem and two leaves, make three long straight stitches with pale green.

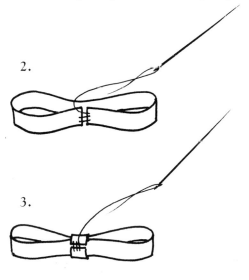

2.

3.

4.

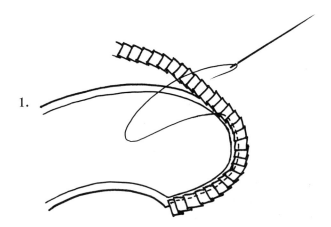

1.

TWIST SKIRT

 FROM THE CLOSET
Knee-length, eight-gore blue-gray skirt

Tip
Make sure the lining of your skirt doesn't show—shorten it if it peeks out!

1. Decorate the gores
Photocopy the template on page 155, enlarging to 200%. If needed, refine the shape to be smaller than but echo the skirt gore. Add a ½" (1 cm) margin all around. Cut it out. Lay the polka-dot fabric wrong-side up and on it, mark around the template eight times (always align the template on the straight grain). Cut out the pieces. Pressing the folds with an iron as you go, turn ½" (1 cm) to the wrong side all around each.

Lay the skirt right-side out so that one gore is flat. Center one of the cut-out overlays on it, aligning at the top. Using pearl cotton, sew the overlay to the gore with irregular running stitches—a bit like seed stitch, but in a line. Repeat with the other gores and overlays.

2. Add stenciled motifs
In the center of the cardboard, draw a circle the same size as the larger round motif on your fabric (or choose a simple motif appropriate to your fabric). Cut out the shape and discard it; the remaining piece is your stencil.

MATERIALS
+ Polka-dot fabric, 48" x 28" (120 x 70 cm): white on dark brown, with large white and beige rounds
+ Stretch tulle, 60" x 8" (150 x 20 cm): red:
+ Sewing thread: blue
+ Pearl cotton, size 5 or 8: black
+ Textile paint: opaque silver
+ Lightweight cardboard: small square for stencil template
+ Plastic bag (to protect garment during painting)

SUPPLIES
+ Basic sewing supplies (see page 149)
+ Embroidery needle
+ Craft knife
+ Stencil brush

Refer to the basic techniques on pages 150–153

Lay the skirt right-side out so one of the gores is flat. Slide the plastic bag between the layers. Using the stencil, paint some silver motifs at random on the overlay and then add a few that trail onto the base fabric, so the pieces seem to merge naturally. For each motif, hold the stencil flat against the fabric, dip the brush in paint and tap the bristles gently over the stencil until the motif is filled; lift the stencil straight up. When you reposition the stencil, make sure it doesn't touch the wet motif. Let the skirt sit until the paint is dry to the touch, then reposition it and repeat on the next gore. Follow the manufacturer's instructions to set the paint.

3. Make a faux petticoat

Cut the tulle into six bands, each 48" x 1¼" (150 x 3 cm). Using a long, doubled thread, sew running stitches close to the long edge of one band. Pull the thread to gather the band into a loose, flirty ruffle, then knot the thread. Repeat with the other bands.

Referring to the photos, pin the bands around the inside of the skirt hem. Arrange them end-to-end, overlapping just a bit, so it looks as though there is a petticoat peeking out. Sew them on from the inside of the skirt; use running stitch and be sure to sew through only the inside layer of the hem so the stitches don't show on the outside.

MONTMARTRE TANK

1. Dress up the straps

Measure one of the straps on your tank top. This length plus 5¼" (13 cm) = L. Cut two strips, each L x 1¼" (L x 3 cm), from each print fabric.

Using an iron, press ¼" (0.5 cm) to the wrong side on each edge of each strip. Then fold each strip in half lengthwise, right-side out; press. Sew the open edges of each strip closed by machine, stitching close to the edge.

Sort the fabric strips into two groups, each with three different prints. Referring to the photos, lay a group over each of the tank straps, letting the ends dangle equally in the front and back. Crisscross the strip ends where the tank straps join the neckline as shown; pin. Try on the tank and adjust the angles of the strips if you need to. Sew across the strips to attach them to the base of each strap—you can sew by hand or machine.

2. Add the buttons

Sew a button over the strips where they crisscross at the base of each strap. Use the larger buttons on the front and the smaller ones on the back.

MATERIALS

- 3 different print fabrics, each 24" x 4" (60 x 10 cm)
- 2 flat wood or plastic vintage buttons, 1" (2.5 cm) in diameter: color to suit your outfit
- 2 flat metal buttons, ¾" (2 cm) in diameter: antique finish
- Sewing thread: black

SUPPLIES

- Basic sewing supplies (see page 149)
- Sewing machine

Refer to the basic techniques on pages 150–153

COED BLOUSE

FROM THE CLOSET
Blue polka-dot blouse with collar, breast pockets and short sleeves gathered into cuffs

1. Prep the blouse

Taking care not to pierce the fabric, remove the collar, pockets and flaps, and buttons from your blouse.

2. Change the neckline

Mark a new round neckline on one of the blouse fronts, placing the base at the center front 4" (10 cm) below the shoulder seam (**drawing 1**). Fold the blouse so the fronts align at the center and shoulders. Pin through both layers and cut along the marked line.

3. Face the new neckline

Prep the facings

Lay the blouse so one front neck is flat on the tracing paper. Draw along the neckline, indicating where the front edge and shoulder seams intersect it. Remove the blouse and draw another line parallel to and 2½" (5 cm) below the first. Mark a vertical line between them at the front edge. Cut the pattern out, leaving a wide margin at the shoulder end. Place the pattern over the blouse and mark the shoulder angl, then trim the pattern on the mark (**drawing 2**). Make a pattern for the back neck facing in the same way.

Lay the patterns on the wrong side of the off-white fabric and mark two front facings (reversing one) and one back facing,

MATERIALS

+ Print fabric, 44" x 16" (110 x 40 cm): brown and blue motifs on off-white
+ Batting, 2½" x 2½" (5 x 5 cm)
+ 30 small mother-of-pearl buttons, assorted types
+ Small pearlized rocaille (tube) beads: white, pale yellow
+ Snaps, to replace the blouse buttons
+ Sewing thread: off-white
+ Tracing paper
+ Lightweight cardboard

SUPPLIES

+ Basic sewing supplies (see page 149)
+ Sewing machine
+ Seam ripper
+ Compass

Refer to the basic techniques on pages 150–153

adding ¾" (2 cm) at the front edge and ½" (1.5 cm) at the shoulders and lower edges. Cut out the facings.

With the right sides together, pin the back facing between the front facings at the shoulders. Sew together at each shoulder, using ½" (1 cm) seam allowance (**drawing 3**). Overcast the lower edge of the facing by hand or with a small zigzag stitch.

Attach the facing
With the right sides together, pin the facing to the blouse neckline. Baste, then sew ¼" (1 cm) from the neck edge.

Turn the facing to the inside of the blouse, clipping the allowance if necessary; press the seam. Fold the allowance under at each front edge (so it's between the facing and blouse placket); press, and whipstitch in place along the front edge.

2.

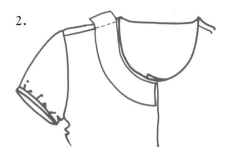

1.

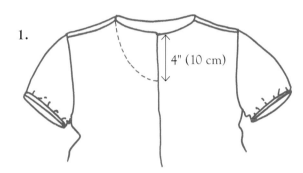

4" (10 cm)

3.

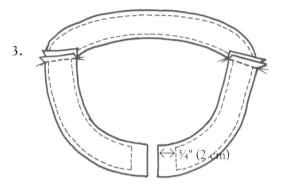

¾" (2 cm)

COED BLOUSE *continued*

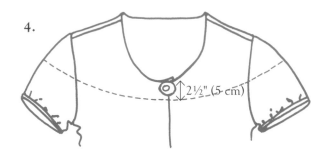

4. ↕ 2½" (5 cm)

4. Give the placket a new look!

Snaps

Sew the buttonholes closed with small whipstitches. On the left front, sew the male half of a snap to the inside of the placket under each buttonhole. Sew the female snaps in the corresponding positions on the right front.

Top button

Draw two circles on the cardboard, one 2½" (6 cm) and one 1¼" (3 cm) in diameter; cut out. Use these templates to cut one large circle from fabric and one small circle from batting.

With your fingers, fold a narrow margin to the wrong side on the fabric circle. With doubled thread, sew a small running stitch all around. Center the small template on the wrong side of this and pull the thread so the edge folds over and gathers in the middle; press a crease around the template edge with your fingers. Loosen the gathering enough to remove the template and replace it with the batting circle. Tighten the gathers again and secure them with a few stitches.

Center this button over the top buttonhole on the left front of the blouse and sew in place, stitching through the gathers.

5. Add a ruffle

Fasten the snaps; lay the blouse flat. Referring to the photos, create a placement line for the ruffle on one of the fronts—insert a line of pins through both layers from center front to the folded edge of the sleeve, adjusting until you like the effect. Mark this line on the front and back with chalk. Make a tracing-paper pattern and use it to transfer this shape to the other half of the blouse (**drawing 4**).

Cut two fabric strips, each 44" x 4½" (110 x 12 cm). Using a narrow seam allowance, sew them together to make one long strip. Using an iron, press ¼" (0.5 cm) to the wrong side on each edge. Then fold the strip in half lengthwise, right-side out; press. Whipstitch each end closed.

Gather the top edge (open edge) of the ruffle by hand. Do one half at a time, using a long doubled thread and making small running stitches close to the open edge through both layers from the closed end to the seam in the middle; leave long thread tails at each end.

Pull the thread to gather the ruffle so it fits along the placement line on the blouse. Pin the ruffle to the line, adjusting the gathers as needed, then knot the gathering thread at each end. Whipstitch the gathered edge of the ruffle to the blouse.

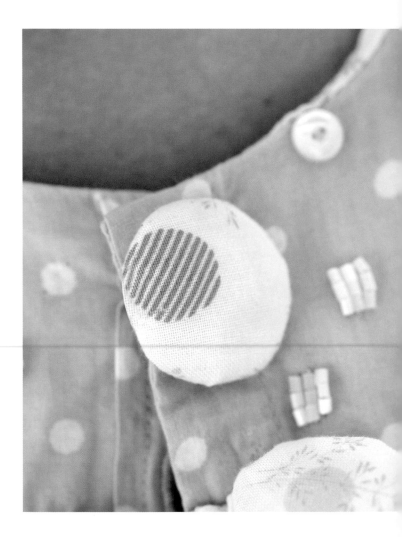

6. Add the embellishments

Sew the buttons and beads at random over some of the polka dots above the ruffle on the blouse front. Refer to the photos and distribute the sizes, shapes and colors harmoniously. Sew the beads in groups of nine to make small squares, as shown.

RETRO

BEAD IT!

FROM THE CLOSET
Tan skirt with a deep yoke and gores alternating with godets

Note
If the dressmaker's carbon paper doesn't give sharp outlines to the motifs when you transfer them to your fabric, refine them with a white fabric pencil.

1. Create the motifs
Photocopy both sets of motifs on page 156.

To transfer a motif to the skirt, lay the dressmaker's carbon ink-side-up, place the desired section of the skirt right-side down on top of it, and then pin the photocopy on the wrong side of the skirt. Draw over the design lines with a stylus or knitting needle. Remove the pattern. Make sure to center each motif between the vertical seams of its panel, with the bottom of the motifs a consistent distance above the hem. Transfer the larger (vertical) motif to each rectangular gore. Transfer the smaller (horizontal) motif to each triangular godet.
  Paint each motif. Let the paint dry. Follow the manufacturer's instructions to set the paint.

Referring to the photos and using pearl cotton, sew black beads along the left edge of each vertical motif; sew nine bronze beads in each large diamond. Sew bronze beads along the top edge of each horizontal motif. Work section by section, knotting and cutting the thread when you finish each.

MATERIALS
- Silk crepe, 44" x 8" (110 x 20 cm): black
- Fusible interfacing, 44" x 4" (110 x 4 cm)
- Small rocaille (tube) beads: shiny black, shiny bronze
- Textile paint: pearlized blue
- Sewing thread: black
- Pearl cotton, size 5 or 8: black
- Dressmaker's carbon paper: white

SUPPLIES
- Basic sewing supplies (see page 149)
- Embroidery needle
- Artist's paintbrushes: small and medium width

Refer to the basic techniques on pages 150–153

2. Make the sash

Make the attached band

The circumference of the skirt at the lower hip (around the bottom of the yoke) = L. From the interfacing, cut a strip measuring L x 1¾" (L x 4 cm). Pin this strip adhesive-side down on the wrong side of the silk. Mark an outline ½" (1 cm) away all around; cut out on this line. Using your iron, bond the interfacing to the silk, then fold and press the margin of silk on each edge onto the interfacing.

Starting and ending at the zipper, pin the band silk-side out, around the bottom of the yoke. Sew all four edges of the band to the skirt with small whipstitches.

Make the bow

From the silk, cut a rectangle measuring 28" x 4" (70 x 10 cm). Fold it in half lengthwise, wrong-side out. Using running stitches, sew the open edges closed as follows: stitch across each end at an angle; on the long edge, leave a ½" (1 cm) seam allowance and leave a 4" (10 cm) opening in the middle. Trim the excess fabric at each end as shown (**drawing below**). Turn the piece right-side out. Fold the seam allowance in at the opening, press and whipstitch closed.

Tie the piece into a pretty bow with unequal tails. Sew it to the sash at the side of the skirt, at the top of a godet.

Latin Quarter tunic

 FROM THE CLOSET

Lightweight red crewneck sweater with long sleeves

1. Restyle the sleeves

Make a pattern

Lay the sweater flat, with the front facing up. Mark a line across each sleeve as shown (**drawing 1**). Make a tracing-paper pattern the size and shape of the area between this line and the armhole seam; mark points A and B on it. On each sleeve, insert a pin at the ends of the marked line.

Turn the sweater over, so the back faces up. Mark a line from pin to pin across the sleeve. Now make a pattern of the top of the back of sleeve. Lay the two patterns on a large sheet of paper, separating them by 5" (12 cm) as shown (**drawing 2**). Tape them down. Extend the top and bottom contours across the gap. Draw a line ½" (1 cm) outside the pattern edges, all around the shape. Cut along this outer line.

Make the new sleeves

Use the pattern to cut two sleeves from the print fabric—be sure to turn the pattern over for the second one. With the wrong-side-out, fold each sleeve in half, bringing the underarm edges together. Pin and then sew by machine between A and B, stitching ½" (1 cm) from the edge. Pressing the folds with an iron as you go, turn ½" (1 cm) to the wrong side along the top and bottom edges. Gather the top and bottom edges of each sleeve by hand. Use a long doubled thread, make small running stitches close to the edge; don't pull the thread up yet, just leave long thread tails at each end.

MATERIALS

+ Geometric print fabric, 21" x 21" (50 x 50 cm): multicolor on white
+ Fabric scraps (for covering buttons)
+ 5 shank button forms (to cover), ⅝" (1.5 cm) in diameter
+ Round elastic, 24" (60 cm)
+ Sewing thread: yellow or green
+ Embroidery floss: light yellow
+ Tracing paper
+ Transparent tape

SUPPLIES

+ Basic sewing supplies (see page 149)
+ Sewing machine
+ Safety pin
+ Embroidery needle

Refer to the basic techniques on pages 150–153

Attach the new sleeves

Turn the new sleeves right-side out. Slide one over each of the sweater sleeves (right over right and left over left); align the underarm seams and place the top edge at the sweater armhole seam and the bottom edge at the marked line. Now pull the gathering threads to fit the top edge of the new sleeve to the sweater. Pin, then whipstitch to the armhole seamline. Fit and attach the bottom edge to the marked line in the same way. Tie off all the gathering threads and pass them to the inside of the sweater.

Cut off the sweater sleeves 1¼" (3 cm) below the marked line. On each sleeve, overcast the edge of this margin; then fold ¾" (2 cm) to the inside for a hem. Sew the hem with invisible stitches, leaving a small opening at the underarm seam. Cut the elastic into two equal pieces. Affix one in the safety pin and thread it through the hem on one sleeve. Repeat for the other sleeve hem. Try the sweater on and pull the elastic tight enough to make the sleeve hems hug your arms; knot the elastic together to secure the size (get a friend to help). Take the sweater off, cut off the excess elastic, feed the knot into each hem and finish sewing the hem at the underarm seam.

2. Trompe-l'œil pockets!

Photocopy the template on page 155. Cut two strips from the print fabric, each 4½" x 1" (11 x 2 cm). Using the iron, press ¼" (0.5 cm) to the wrong side on each edge of each strip. Pin the strips to the sweater front, placing them about 7" (17 cm) above the bottom and centered about 5" (12 cm) apart. Whipstitch the strips to the sweater. Place the pocket template below each strip and draw around it with chalk. Using two strands of floss, embroider the outline in backstitch.

3. Chic detail: covered buttons

Follow the package instructions to cover 5 buttons, each with a different fabric. Sew one to the sweater below each faux pocket welt. Sew the three others in a vertical line at the center front, just below the neckband as shown.

1.

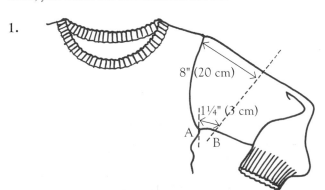

8" (20 cm)

1¼" (3 cm)

A   B

2.

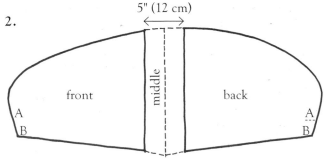

5" (12 cm)

front   middle   back

A
B

A
B

DIVA

Coquette dress

It takes only a few details to give an ordinary dress wild allure: to intensify the deep black of the gauzy dress, a scattering of cloth pastilles in subtle colors; to catch the light, a dusting of sequins over the bust; to draw the eye, a small, flirtatious bright red bow.
Instructions p. 128

Belle Époque blouson

A vertical overlay of fabric strips gives new structure to a simple tank top and accents your silhouette. Here's to quiet femininity well played!
Instructions p. 130

114

Traviata bolero
It's child's play to add a little punch to a dull sweater. Just weave some fabric through the knit sleeves and accent with butterfly bows. For a true couture finish, accent your work with sparkling jet-black beads.
Instructions p. 134

Tiffany tunic
Style can be effortless! This tunic proves it: the black silk yo-yos that edge the neckline elegantly reinterpret the dot motif of the fabric and highlight the bust.
Instructions p. 136

Carmen cami

Transform a tank top that has a sporty cut into one with an air of refinement: wrap the neck and armhole edges with a narrow band of print fabric, add flirty cap sleeves made of yo-yos fashioned from the same print, sew some flower cutouts and a shower of glittery black beads to one strap.... *Instructions p. 138*

120

Mad for plaid

Go ahead, adopt that dry sense of humor for which the Brits are famous. The recipe: mix a classic wool plaid with fluorescent-colored tulle and sprinkle with a few beads. The result: You can't help but smile—even on days when you feel a little blue.
Instructions p. 140

Sweet nothings
Begin with a simple wrap dress, end up with something totally irresistible! Take a cue from the elegance of yesteryear to embellish the neckline with a cascading bouquet of cloth flowers. Sew them on carefully so as not to spoil the delicacy of their full bloom.
Instructions p. 142

125

Dolce Vita bustier
There's nothing like a splash of water to fight off summer's heat, so appliqué some large drops across the front of a black tank top. Give it new straps, too, embroidering them with a stream of beads and topping with fountain of pleats. Deliciously chilled!
Instructions p. 144

DIVA

Coquette dress

From the closet
Lined black polyester voile dress with smocked waist and skinny straps

Tip

When you are ready to add the embellishments, slide a cushion inside the dress bodice. This will give it some shape so you can judge the effect of your arrangement. But be sure not to sew the dress to the cushion!

1. Yo-yos for zest

Draw a circle 1½" (4 cm) in diameter on the cardboard. Cut this out for a template, then trace around it nine times on the blue fabric and five times on the figured fabric. Cut out the circles.

Referring to page 153 and using an iron, fold and press a narrow margin to the wrong side around each circle. Then, with matching thread used double, sew a running stitch parallel to the edge all around. Pull the thread to gather the fabric as tightly as possible, then knot and cut the thread. Flatten the yo-yos so the gathers are in the center of one side.

Pin the yo-yos to the smocked section on the front of the dress (below the bust), arranging in a loose, pleasing pattern. Sew them on, stitching over the smocking thread and knotting and cutting your thread on the inside after attaching each.

MATERIALS

+ Plain fabric, 8" x 4"
(20 x 10 cm): midnight blue
+ Figured fabric, 8" x 2"
(20 x 5 cm): blue on white
+ Stretch tulle, 12" x ¼"
(30 x 0.7 cm): red (or red satin ribbon)
+ Sequins, size 1 cm (off-center hole): translucent yellow, translucent blue
+ Sewing thread: color to match dress and fabrics
+ Lightweight cardboard

SUPPLIES

+ Basic sewing supplies
(see page 149)
+ Compass
Refer to the basic techniques on pages 150–153

2. Sequins for flair

Sew sequins to the bodice above the smocking. Orient the sequins so the hole is at the top; sew them on individually with a few vertical stitches, always knotting and cutting the thread after attaching each one. Distribute the two colors equally over the bodice.

3. A bow for charm

Referring to the photo, tie a bow in the tulle. Sew it to the center front just below the neckline, attaching with a few small stitches.

DIVA

Belle Époque blouson

From the closet
Off-white tank top with skinny straps and gathered center-front neckline, finished at the bottom with a deep band or hem

Tip
Use a bodkin or tube turner (from the notions section of your fabric store) to quickly turn the vertical bands right-side out.

1. Add vertical bands

Lay the tank top flat, right-side out, with the front facing up. Draw a line across it from side seam to side seam, about 3" (7 cm) below the neckband. The length of this line = L. The distance from this line to the top of the hem band plus ½" (1 cm) = H. To figure the number of bands you need to cut, divide L by ⅝" (1.5 cm) and round down; the result = N.

Cut N bands from the floral fabric, making each H x 1½" (H x 3 cm). Fold each band in half lengthwise, wrong-side out. Sew the long open edge of each closed, using a ¼" (0.5 cm) seam allowance. Turn each band right-side out (affix the safety pin at one end and push it through the tube). Then manipulate the seam so it is in the middle of one side, not at the edge; press. At each end, turn in ¼" (0.5 cm) and whipstitch closed.

Attach the bands
Divide the guideline marked on the tank top into four equal sections, marking each by inserting a pin across it. Repeat at the top of the hem band. Pin the bands to the top of the hem

MATERIALS

+ Floral print fabric, 44" x 20" (110 x 50 cm): marine blue on ecru
+ Silk crepe, black: 20" x 12" (50 x 30 cm)
+ Sewing thread: black, ecru

SUPPLIES

+ Basic sewing supplies (see page 149)
+ Sewing machine
+ Safety pin

Refer to the basic techniques on pages 150–153

band, arranging them so they hang down, with the seam on each facing up (**drawing 1**). Space them at regular intervals between the vertical pins. Whipstitch the end of each to the top of the hem. Then lift each band and align its other end on the top guideline. Check that each one is perfectly vertical. Whipstitch the top end of each strip to the guideline.

2. Add top trim

Add ½" (1 cm) to L. Cut a band this length and 1" (2.5 cm) wide from the black silk. With your iron, press ¼" (0.5 cm) to the wrong side on all four edges. Pin the band right-side up across the front of the tank top, covering the top ends of the vertical bands. Whipstitch in place on all edges.

1.

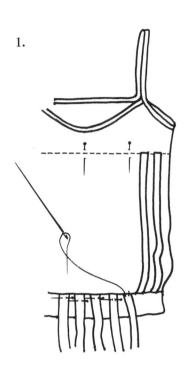

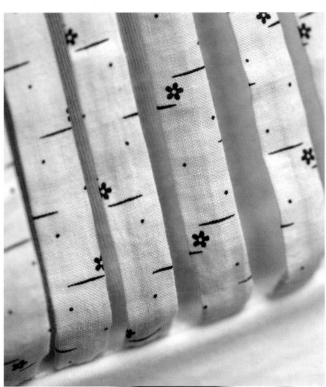

Belle Époque blouson continued

2.

3.

top

4.

bottom

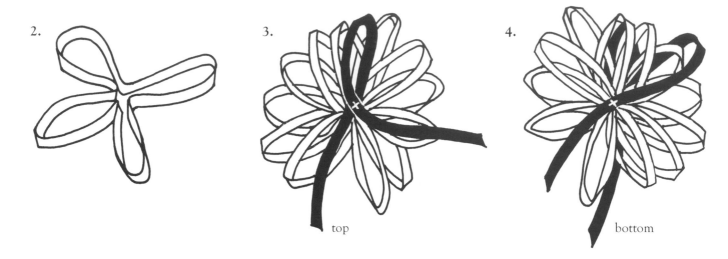

3. Make the flower

Cut four strips from the black silk, each 20" x 1½" (50 x 3 cm). Fold each in half lengthwise, wrong-side out. Sew the long open edge of each closed, using ¼" (0.5 cm) seam allowance. Turn the bands right-side out. At each end, turn in ¼" (0.5 cm) and whipstitch closed. Press.

Manipulate one of the bands to form four equal loops radiating from a central point (**drawing 2**). Join the loops with a few stitches at the center. Do the same with two more bands. Superimpose the three units one on the other, offsetting the loops, and join at the center with a few stitches through all layers. Place the remaining band on top of this unit. Leaving 4¾" (12 cm) loose at one end, form a loop and secure at the center (**drawing 3**). Wrap the remainder of the band around the flower to form one more loop and secure on the back (**drawing 4**). Sew the flower to the tank top at the midpoint of the black band.

4. Embellish the straps

Make two more bands of print fabric identical to the ones sewn vertically to the tank front, but don't finish their ends. Cut each of these into seven tabs, each 1½" (3 cm) long. Tuck in and whipstitch each end of each tab.

From the silk, cut two strips, each 4¾" x 1½" (12 x 3 cm). Using the iron, press ¼" (0.5 cm) to the wrong side on one long edge and both ends. Hem the ends with invisible stitches. Fold each strip in half crosswise and insert a pin across it to mark the midpoint.

Lay the tank top flat, aligning the bottom edge on the front and back and smoothing upward. Place a pin across each strap where it folds. Pick up the tank so you can unfold the straps.

Wrap one of the silk strips around one of the straps, aligning the pins and overlapping the silk on the back of the strap so that its raw edge is covered (**drawing 5**). Whipstitch the strip to itself, catching the strap in the stitches as you go. As shown in the drawing and photos, arrange seven of the small floral print tabs on the underside of the strap so they extend toward the armhole: center one on the pin and place three on each side of it. Whipstitch them to the strap. Embellish the other strap in the same way.

5.

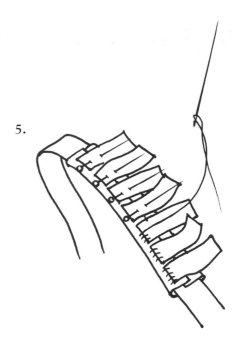

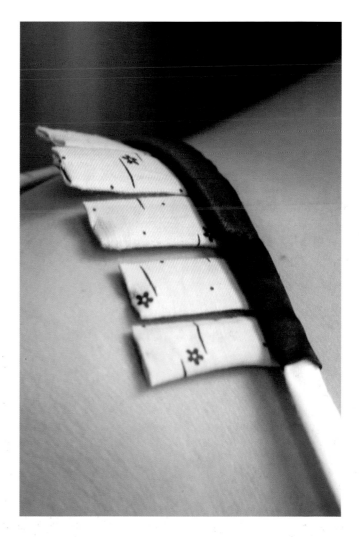

DIVA

Traviata bolero

From the closet
Purple knit bolero with shawl collar and long sleeves

MATERIALS

+ Checkerboard fabric, 44" x 4"
(110 x 10 cm): mustard yellow,
black, tan, and purple
+ Paisley fabric, 44" x 4"
(110 x 10 cm): light yellow and
blue on deep lavender
+ Small rocaille (tube) beads:
shiny black
+ Sewing thread: black

SUPPLIES

+ Basic sewing supplies
(see page 149)
+ Sewing machine
+ Safety pin
+ Yarn needle (large
eye, blunt point)

**Refer to the basic
techniques on pages
150–153**

1. Add the bows

Make the bows
From the checkerboard fabric cut a strip measuring 36" x 3¼" (90 x 8 cm). Also cut six rectangles, each 1" x 1 ⅝" (2.5 x 4 cm).

Fold the long strip in half lengthwise, wrong-side-out. Sew the long open edge closed, leaving a ¼" (0.5 cm) seam allowance. Turn right-side out. Cut the strip into six pieces, each 6" (15 cm) long.

One at a time, fold each piece in half crosswise and mark the midpoint; then unfold and form into a loop, overlapping the ends slightly opposite the mark. Using doubled thread, secure the loop with running stitches made through all layers (**drawing 1**). Pull the thread to gather the layers as tightly as possible, then secure with a few stitches; knot and cut.

For the bow knots, press a narrow margin to the wrong side on both long edges of each of the small rectangles and hem with invisible stitch. Wrap one, right-side out, around the middle of each loop; overlap the ends and secure with a few stitches (**drawing 2**).

Bead the bow knots
Sew a few beads to each bow knot, placing them at random, singly or in small groups.

Attach the bows

Referring to the photos, sew one bow to the top of each bolero sleeve, right at the end of the shoulder seam. Then sew two more below the first, spacing them about 2" (5 cm) apart.

2. Weave in a trim

From the paisley fabric cut three strips, each 44" x 1¼" (110 x 3 cm). Using the iron, press ¼" (0.5 cm) to the wrong side on both long edges of each strip. Then fold each strip in half lengthwise, right-side out; press. Sew the open edges of each strip closed by machine, stitching close to the edge.

Use the yarn needle to weave the trims through the sleeves as shown in the photos and drawing: for the top row, begin and end at the underarm seam and weave right along the armhole seam. Weave very loosely and insert the needle in and out at ¾" (2 cm) intervals. Cut the excess trim on the inside and, using regular sewing thread, join the ends with a few small stitches. In this manner, weave a second row of trim parallel to the first, spacing it to pass under the second bow; this time begin and end opposite the second stitch from the underarm seam; cut the excess and whipstitch each end to the inside of the sleeve. Weave a third, shorter row, spacing it to pass under the third bow (**drawing 3**).

3. Add bead embroidery

Embroider small bead rectangles between the woven trim stitches. For each, sew three vertical rows of three beads each; then sew one horizontal row of three beads above them and another below them (**drawing 4**). Work the rectangles individually, using doubled sewing thread and knotting and cutting the thread after finishing each one.

1.

2.

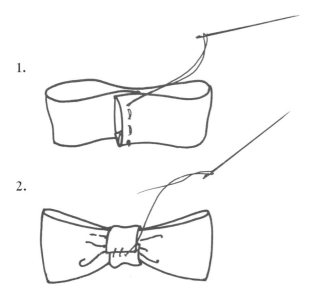

3.

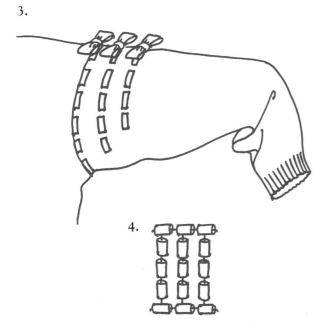

4.

Tiffany tunic

shown on page 118

From the closet
Oversize tunic with deep V-neck, in a stylized
black-and-white-dot print

Tip
On the sample garment shown in the photos, the yo-yos are
all affixed smooth-side up, with their gathers face-down. But
you might like them gathered-side up, or even choose to
alternate their orientation—these options produce an interesting
effect, especially if the gathers are neatly done. If you decide
to arrange the yo-yos with the gathers facing up, sew them on
through the smooth layer only.

1. Make the yo-yos
Draw two circles on the cardboard, one 4¼" (11 cm) and one
2" (5 cm) in diameter; cut out.
 Measure the distance around the neckline of your tunic.
Divide this length by 2" (5 cm); the result is the number of
yo-yos you need. Using the larger of the two templates as a
pattern, cut that many circles from the black silk.

Referring to page 153 and using your fingers, fold a narrow
margin to the wrong side on one of the fabric circles. With
doubled thread, sew a small running stitch all around. Center
the small template on the wrong side of this and pull the
thread so the edge folds over and gathers in the middle; press
a crease around the template edge with your fingers. Loosen
the gathering enough to remove the template, then pull the
thread tight again and knot it securely. Repeat for each circle.

MATERIALS

+ Silk crepe, 24" x 20"
(60 x 50 cm): black
+ Sewing thread: black
+ Lightweight cardboard

SUPPLIES

+ Basic sewing supplies
(see page 149)
+ Compass

**Refer to the basic
techniques on pages
150–153**

2. Sew on the yo-yos

Pin the yo-yos one next to the other around the neck, lapping them over the edge as shown. Sew each one on from the wrong side, stitching through the gathers only and securing the thread with a backstitch before proceeding to the next one.

Carmen cami

From the closet
Brick-color ribbed tank top

Tip
Try the tank top on and measure the neckline and armhole edges. Make the bindings in these lengths (finished length)—you can stretch the tank edges when you pin on the bindings.

1. Bind the edges
Cut two strips from the print fabric, each 44" x 1" (110 x 2.5 cm). Using your iron, press ¼" (0.5 cm) to the wrong side on both long edges of each strip.

Starting and ending at one shoulder seam, fold one strip over the neck edge, right-side out, and pin in place. Leaving enough to turn under at each end, cut off the excess. Turn the ends under. Whipstitch the strip edge to the right side of the tank, then to the wrong side, and sew the ends together neatly. Add a binding to each armhole in the same way, starting and ending at the underarm seam.

2. Add yo-yo sleeve caps
Draw a circle 3¼" (8 cm) in diameter on the cardboard; cut it out. Using this template as a pattern, cut 22 circles from the print fabric.

MATERIALS
+ Floral print fabric, 44" x 12" (110 x 30 cm): pink-red-and-white on black
+ Seed beads: shiny black
+ Sewing thread: black
+ Lightweight cardboard

SUPPLIES
+ Basic sewing supplies (see page 149)
+ Compass

Refer to the basic techniques on pages 150–153

Referring to page 153 and using an iron, fold and press a narrow margin to the wrong side around each circle. Then, with doubled thread, sew a running stitch parallel to the edge all around. Pull the thread to gather the fabric as tightly as possible, then knot and cut the thread. Flatten the yo-yos so the gathers are in the center of one side, but don't press—you want to preserve the dimension of the gathers.

Sew two yo-yos together side-by-side, joining with a small secure stitch; slide the needle across one of these yo-yos, between the layers, and attach another. Continuing in this way, assemble two rows of eight yo-yos and two rows of three yo-yos. Then sew each short row to the center of one long row as shown below. Pin one of the assembled units to each armhole with the gathers facing the right side, as shown, centering the long edge on the shoulder seam and tucking the yo-yos under the armhole edge. Whipstitch the yo-yos to the armhole binding on the inside of the tank top.

3. Appliqué some flowers
Choose three flower motifs from the fabric (for example, two small and one large bloom). Cut out, adding a small margin all around each shape. Sew a running stitch around the edge of each and pull the thread just enough to turn the margin to the wrong side; press lightly. Arrange the flowers on the tank top at the base of one strap and whipstitch in place.

4. Shower with beads!
Referring to the photo, sew a scattering of beads over the strap with the flowers. Use doubled thread, and carry it from bead to bead on the wrong side, being sure to keep it loose so the fabric doesn't buckle. Begin at the top of the strap, along the shoulder seam, arranging the beads fairly densely. As you work down toward the flowers, gradually increase the space between the beads.

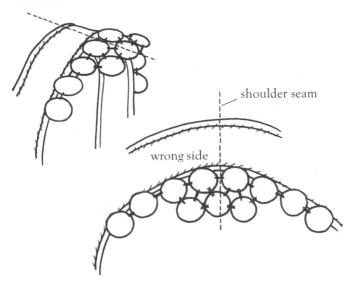

shoulder seam

wrong side

Mad for plaid

From the closet
Gray plaid (Prince of Wales) cropped pants, cuffed below the knee

1. Accent with petite frills

Cut two strips from the plaid fabric, each 10" x 3" (25 x 10 cm). Pressing the folds with the iron as you go, turn ¼" (1 cm) to the wrong side on all four edges of each strip. Then press ½" (2 cm) to the wrong side on each long edge; hem the long edges with whipstitches.

Referring to the photos, fold and press knife pleats into each strip, parallel to the ends. Make the pleats on one strip face the opposite direction from those on the other strip. Turn each strip wrong-side up and secure the pleats along the top edge with small overcast stitches, trying not to go through to the right side.

From each color tulle, cut two strips, each 10" x 1¾" (25 x 4 cm). One at a time, make each into a ruffle; use doubled thread to sew running stitches close to one long edge. Pull the thread to gather the edge so it is the same length as the pleated plaid strip; knot and cut the thread.

Referring to the photos, center a fuchsia ruffle across the outside seam of one pant leg, placing its bottom (not gathered) edge a short distance above the bottom edge of the cuff. Pin, then sew it on with open backstitch along the top gathers.

MATERIALS

- Plaid fabric, 10" x 8" (25 x 20 cm): gray-and-white
- Stretch tulle, 10" x 3½" (25 x 8 cm) each: black, red and fuchsia
- Small rocaille (tube) beads: shiny bronze
- Sewing thread: black

SUPPLIES

- Basic sewing supplies (see page 149)

Refer to the basic techniques on pages 150–153

In the same way, add a red ruffle and then a black ruffle over the fuchsia one, placing the top of each one a little higher on the leg to reveal some of the color under it. Add the pleated plaid strip on top in the same way but whipstitch it in place. Repeat this process to decorate the other leg.

2. Add bead embroidery
Referring to the photos, sew beads above each frill: Use doubled thread to sew six vertical lines of seven beads each, spacing them regularly on each side of the seam. Knot and cut the thread after completing each line.

Sweet nothings

From the closet

Wrap-front V-neck dress, off-white with black polka dots, with gathered short sleeves.

Tip

Lavish attention on your fabric bouquet: Experiment with the way the pieces overlap the neckline and each other to create the prettiest effect. Sew each piece on carefully and leave dangling ends loose—you want the bouquet to be firmly attached yet appear to be full of movement and spontaneity.

1. Make the flowers

The centers

Draw a circle 2" (5 cm) in diameter on the cardboard; cut it out. Using this template as a pattern, cut five circles from whichever fabrics you'd like to be the flower centers. With your fingers, fold a narrow margin to the wrong side on one circle. With double thread, sew short running stitches all around. Pull the thread so the edge starts to gather; tuck a small ball of stuffing into the pouch that forms. Pull the thread to close the pouch, forming a compact ball. Knot the thread and cut off the excess. Repeat with the other circles.

The petals

From the fabrics chosen to be the petals, cut one strip measuring 16½" x 3¼" (41 x 7 cm), and four strips, each 12½" x 2" (31 x 5 cm). Using an iron, press ¼" (0.5 cm) to the wrong side on all four edges of each strip. Then fold each strip in

MATERIALS

+ Floral fabrics, scraps of twelve different prints: faded hues
+ Sewing thread: ecru
+ Polyester stuffing
+ Lightweight cardboard

SUPPLIES

+ Basic sewing supplies (see page 149)
+ Compass

Refer to the basic techniques on pages 150–153

half lengthwise, right-side out; press. Working on one strip at a time and using doubled thread, sew running stitches close to each long edge: on the open edge, pull the thread to gather the fabric as tightly as possible, then knot and cut the thread. On the folded edge, pull the thread gently to create soft undulations as shown in the photos.

Assembly
One at a time, roll each petal strip into a spiral with the tight gathers at its base, ready to hold a flower center. Secure the shape with a few stitches through the base; don't cut the thread. Tuck a flower center inside as shown, and sew it in place through the gathers; knot and cut the thread.

2. Make the foliage

The stems
From the fabrics chosen to be stems, cut four strips, each 6½" x ¾" (16 x 2 cm). On each, press a narrow margin under on all four sides and then press in half lengthwise as you did for the petals. Using doubled thread, sew the open edge of each closed with running stitches; pull the thread just enough to make the edge undulate gently. Knot and cut the thread.

The leaves
Using the round template as a pattern, cut eight circles from the fabrics chosen to be leaves.
  Turn under and gather the edge of each circle as you did for the flower centers, but don't stuff them. Instead, flatten each circle so the gathers are in the center of one side; make a few stitches to flatten the gathers.

Attach the leaves to the stems
Referring to the photos, fold a leaf in half, smooth-side-out, and slide it over the end of a stem. Sew the leaf to the stem and then sew the open edges of the leaf together. Sew a leaf to the other end of this stem. Sew the remaining leaves to the other stem ends in the same way.

3. Bouquet!
Arrange the flowers and foliage along one side of the neckline. Place the largest flower about 4" (10 cm) below the shoulder seam and arrange three smaller ones just below it. Fold two of the stems crosswise so the leaves hang at different levels, then tuck the folds under the flowers. Place the remaining flower a short distance below these, then fold and tuck the remaining stems under it. When you are pleased with the arrangement, sew on each element individually, knotting and cutting the thread before proceeding to the next element.

Dolce Vita bustier

From the closet
Black tank top with skinny straps and gathered center-front neckline

MATERIALS

+ Geometric print fabric, 44" x 20" (110 x 50 cm): blue-red-and-black on white
+ Assorted rocaille (tube) beads: orange, red and red-and-orange striped
+ Sewing thread: black
+ Dressmaker's carbon paper: white
+ Lightweight cardboard

SUPPLIES

+ Basic sewing supplies (see page 149)
+ Sewing machine

Refer to the basic techniques on pages 150–153

1. Add motifs

Mark and cut

Photocopy the design on page 160, enlarging to 200% (piece copies together as needed to make a whole design). Photocopy the four motifs on page 159 at 100%. Lay the tank top flat with the front facing up. Lay the carbon paper over it, ink-side-down. Place the design on top as shown; pin. To transfer the design, trace along the lines with a stylus. Remove the papers.

Cut out the four motifs. Draw around each on the cardboard, label the drawing with its letter, and cut out for a template. Cut the following pieces from the fabric, marking each on the wrong side of the fabric and adding a small allowance all around before cutting:
- 8 of motif A, turning the template letter-side-down for 6
- 6 of motif B, turning the template letter-side-down for 2
- 6 of motif C, turning the template letter-side-down for 2
- 3 of motif D

Prep

With doubled thread, sew a short running stitch close to the edge all around one of the cutouts. Center its template on the wrong side of cutout and pull the thread so the fabric folds over the template; press the crease with your iron. Loosen the gathering enough to remove the template, then pull the thread so the margin lies flat again; tie off. Repeat for each cutout.

Appliqué

Pin the cutouts in place on the tank top (slide a piece of cardboard inside so you go through only one layer). Whipstitch each motif in place; knot and cut the thread after each.

2. Dress up the straps

Prep

The length of a strap on the tank top = L. Draw a rectangle measuring L x 1½" (L x 4 cm). Taper the ends as shown below (**drawing 1**). Draw another outline ¼" (0.5 cm) outside this. Cut out on the outer line. Use this pattern to cut four straps from the print fabric.

Place the straps right-sides together in pairs, aligning the edges. Sew the long edges of each, leaving a ¼" (0.5 cm) seam allowance; leave an opening for turning on one edge of each. Turn the straps right-side out. On each, turn in the allowances at the side opening and at each end. Leave the ends open but whipstitch the side closed. Press.

Attach

Cut off the straps on the tank top about ½" (1 cm) above the neck/armhole intersection. Slide the open ends of the new straps over these "stubs." Whipstitch the new straps to the old on both the outside and inside of the tank.

3. Make the fan trims

From the print fabric, cut two strips, each 18" x 2" (43 x 9 cm). Fold each in half lengthwise, wrong-side out. Leaving a ¼" (0.5 cm) seam allowance, sew the long open edge and one end of each closed. Turn the strips right-side out; tuck in the allowance at the open ends and whipstitch each closed.

Referring to the photos and drawing, pleat each strip accordion-style, making the pleats 1¼" (3 cm) deep. Whipstitch the pleats together through all layers at the edge with the strip ends, forming a fan of loops (**drawing 2**).

Lay the tank top flat, aligning the bottom edge on the front and back and smoothing upward. Place a pin across each strap where it folds. Pick up the tank so you can unfold the straps. Referring to the photos, sew a fan trim to each strap at the pin; sew all the way across each strap, through the fan base.

4. Beads: an indispensable final flourish

Sew beads to the front of each strap. Arrange them randomly but orient them along the lines of your print fabric. Start at the base of the strap and decrease the density of the pattern as you work toward the fan. Slide the needle from bead to bead between the layers of the strap so no threads are exposed on the back.

1.

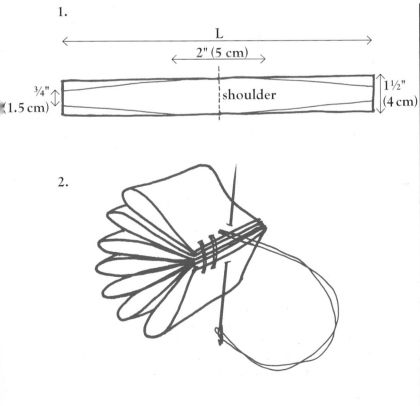

2.

Supplies & techniques

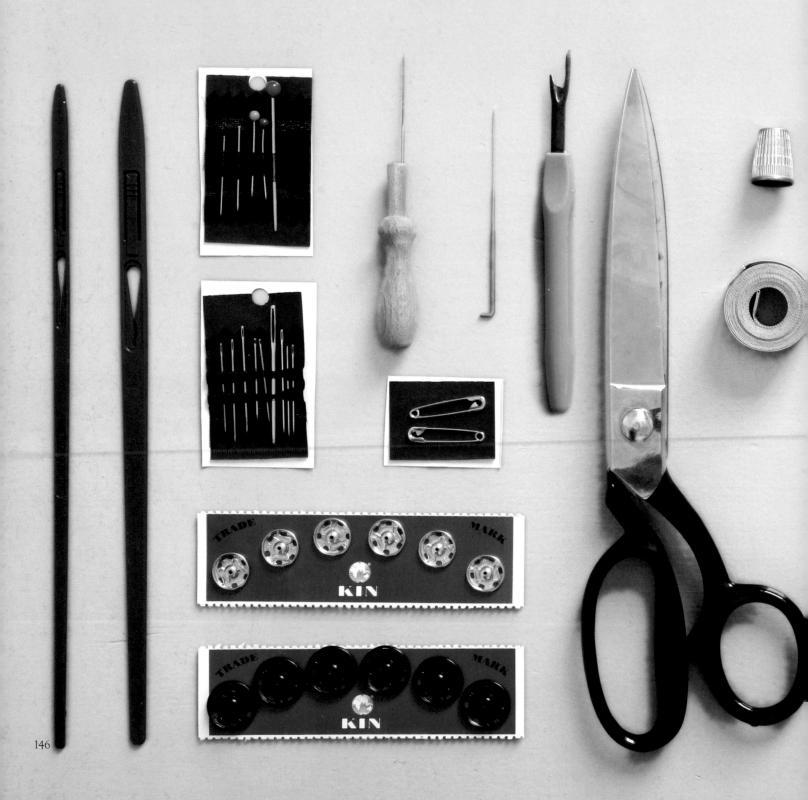

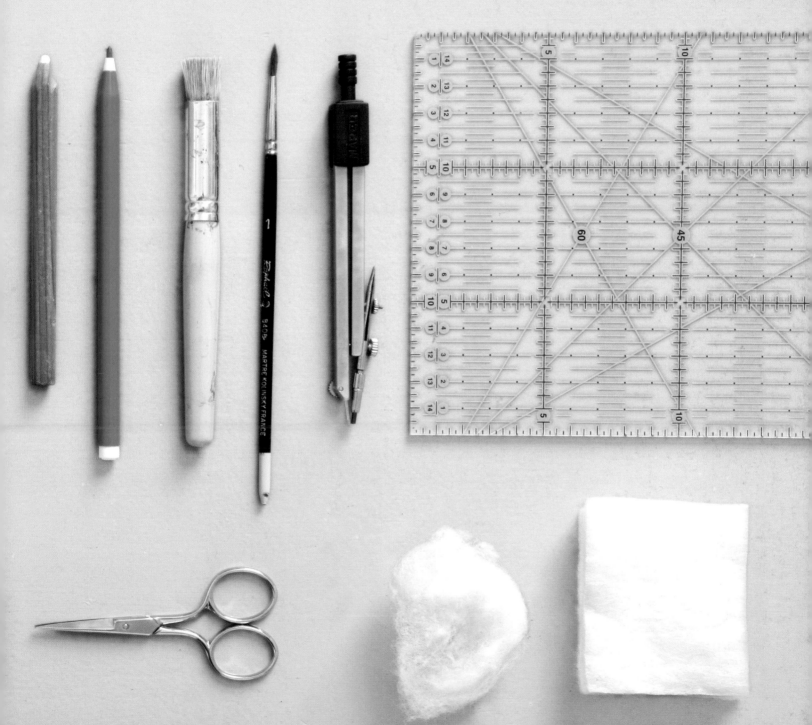

Materials

Fabrics

For most of the embellishments a fine, closely woven cotton fabric is a good choice. This shapes well, pleats and folds neatly, and creates good bindings, appliqués and frills. Quilting fabrics are often perfect because they come in coordinating prints. For softer details you can use a more fluid fabric, such as tulle or silk crepe.

Thread

Choose good-quality sewing thread, preferably cotton. When sewing by machine, or if you want a particularly inconspicuous seam, use a color that matches your fabric. On the other hand, you might wish to deliberately play with contrast effects by sewing your embellishments with differently colored thread.

The projects in this book are often accented with cotton embroidery thread—either pearl cotton or six-strand embroidery floss. You're encouraged to adapt the designs by using a different thread from the one indicated—for instance—you can replace an embroidery thread with sewing thread used double, or vice versa. There's no one way to embellish—it's a matter of taste, tactile sensibility and preferred visual effect.

Beads, sequins and buttons

Give your creativity free reign! Don't hesitate to use whatever treasures you have in your stash, find in trim shops and crafts stores, or unearth at the flea market.

Diverse trims and notions

Some of the projects call for ribbon, lace, batting, interfacing, snap or hook-and-eye fasteners, and dressmaker's carbon paper. You should be able to find all of these items at a fabric store or online vendor.

Supplies

To make any of the projects in this book, you'll need some basic sewing supplies:
- Tape measure
- Ruler
- Pencil
- Non-permanent fabric marker—either ink or chalk. For both types, have on hand both a light color and a dark one, so that you'll be able to place contrast marks on both light- and dark-colored fabrics.
- Dressmaker's shears, for cutting fabric
- Embroidery scissors, for trimming threads and cutting small elements
- Dressmaker's pins or round-head pins
- Sewing needles in assorted sizes
- Basting thread
- Iron and ironing board

Other supplies are listed with each project as needed.

A sewing machine is needed for some of the projects, especially if there are long seams involved. For other projects, you can use a machine if you are comfortable doing so instead of sewing by hand as instructed.

Here are some tips for selecting embroidery needles: The eye should be large enough to hold the thread without causing it to break or fray. Use *embroidery* needles (with a sharp point) for embellishing fabric, but use *tapestry* or *yarn* needles (with a blunt point) when embellishing a sweater knit. Use a long, thin sewing needle (called *milliner's*) to attach beads—*beading* needles are not sufficiently strong to pierce most fabrics.

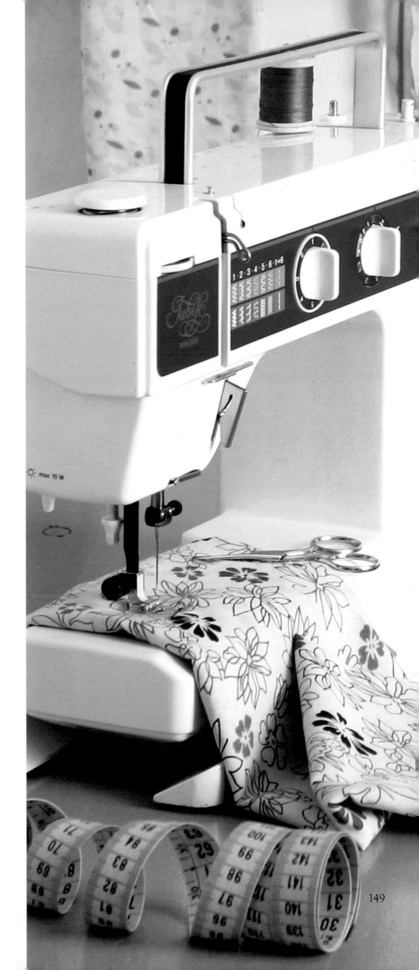

Techniques

Sewing by hand
Tie a knot in the thread end before you sew.

To secure the thread at the end of a seam (or when you run out), make several small backstitches in one place, or make a knot against the fabric surface.

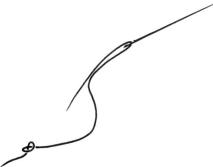

When you work with embroidery thread, secure it by passing under the last few stitches made, then cut it close to the fabric.

Hand-sewing stitches
Running stitch
Work from right to left. Bring the needle up at 1, insert it at 2, and bring it up again at 3. Continue in this fashion, making the stitches the same length on both sides of the work.

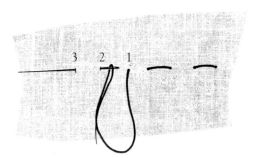

Open backstitch
Work from right to left. Bring the needle up at 1, move it back to the right and insert at 2, and bring it up again at 3. Move the needle to the right again and insert it halfway between 1 and 3. Bring the needle up again to the left of 3—the stitch on the back should be the length of 2 to 3. Continue in this fashion.

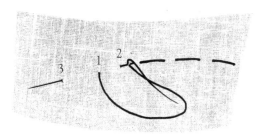

Closed backstitch
This stitch emulates a machine straight stitch. Work from right to left. Bring the needle up at 1, move it back to the right and insert at 2, and bring it up again at 3. Insert it again at 1, then bring it up again to the left of 3. Now insert the needle at 3. Continue to make overlapping straight stitches in this fashion.

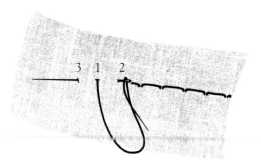

Whipstitch
Use this for appliqué, to attach small elements, and to close an opening in a seam. Work from right to left. Make small angled stitches very close to the edge of the work.

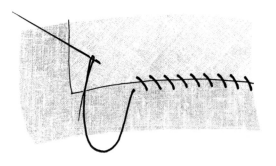

Invisible stitches

Use this for hemming. Work with the wrong side of the hem up, stitching from right to left. Bring the needle up through the fold of the hem, then make a tiny stitch in the main fabric, slightly to the left, above the fold. Continuing to move left, take a stitch through the fold and another through the main fabric. Continue, making the smallest possible stitches on the main fabric so they won't show from the right side.

Swing tack

Use this to attach one element to another while allowing them some freedom to move independently. Bring the needle up at 1; take a stitch through the piece to be joined at 2; leave a link of thread between 1 and 2 (it can be whatever length makes sense for your work). Stitch through 2 again to secure the thread. Now, following the drawings, cover the link with small stitches, working back to 1. Secure the thread at 1.

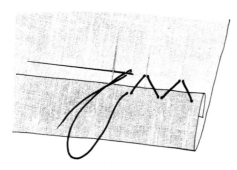

Overcast stitch

Use this to join superimposed pieces right along their edges. Work from right to left. Make small, angled stitches over the edge of the work, piercing both layers with the needle.

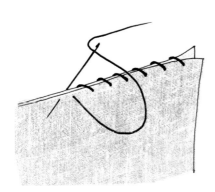

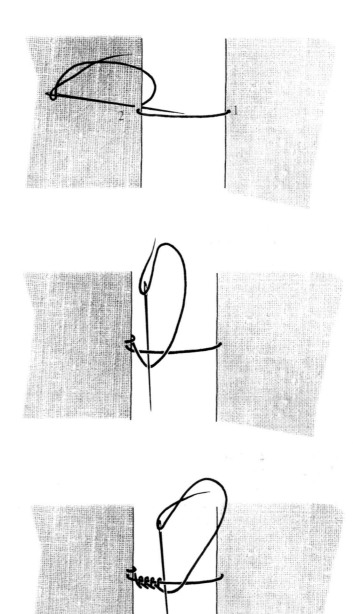

Tip

Some hand-sewing stitches are effective as embroidery stitches: running stitch, open backstitch and whipstitch.

Embroidery stitches

Straight stitch

Make long straight stitches, similar to running stitches, but vary their length and orientation to create a desired effect.

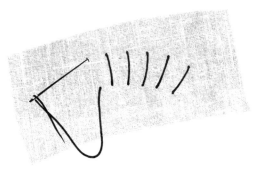

Stem stitch

Work from left to right, keeping the thread below the needle. Bring the needle up at 1, move it to the right and insert from 2 to 3. Continue, making stitches of equal length and always bringing the needle up just above the prior insertion point.

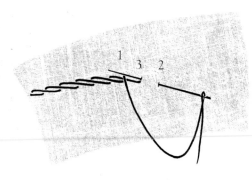

Seeding stitch

Make small straight stitches of equal length, orienting them at random to lightly cover the background.

Lazy daisy stitch

Bring the needle up at 1. Lay the thread against the fabric in a loop and insert the needle at 1, then bring it up inside the thread loop at 2. Pull the thread through and, inserting the needle at 3, take a small stitch over the loop.

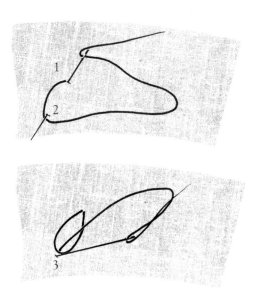

French knot

Bring the needle up at 1. Hold it close to the fabric and wrap the thread around it several times. Hold the thread to keep the wraps tight and reinsert the needle close to 1. Pull the needle all the way through, keeping the tension on the wraps until the knot is nicely formed. The more times you wrap the thread around the needle, the larger the knot will be.

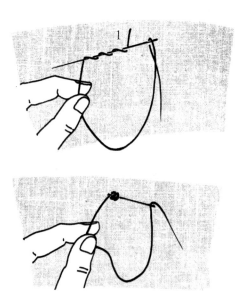

Yo-yos

Cut a fabric circle with a diameter twice that of the desired finished size. Fold a narrow margin to the wrong side. Using doubled thread and stitching through both layers, sew a running stitch all the way around the edge. Pull the thread to gather the edge; flatten the pouch that forms into a disc with the gathers in the middle of one side; tie off the threads. Use this technique to cover buttons or make fabric beads, too.

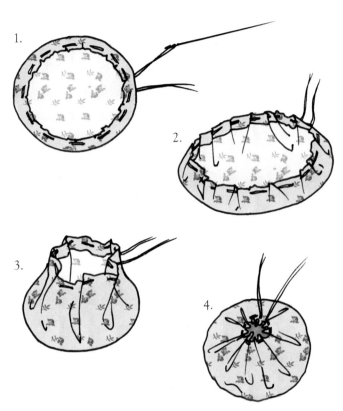

To make a row of overlapping sequins, work from right to left. Sew on the first sequin with a backstitch, bringing the needle up to the left, where the left edge of the next sequin will be once it overlaps the first. Position the next sequin and insert the needle through its hole. Continue in this manner. Secure the thread on the wrong side after attaching the final sequin.

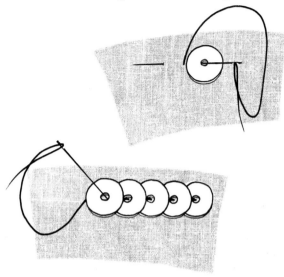

Felted wool embellishments

Use wool roving and a felting needle, both of which you'll find at yarn and craft stores (there are kits with everything you need and detailed instructions, too). Lay the area of fabric you want to embellish right-side-up over a block of Styrofoam. Place a tuft of roving on top. Poke the felting needle repeatedly through the roving and fabric to meld them; the roving fibers will mat together. You can add more roving to create whatever shape you like. The embellished garments can be washed in cold water.

A final touch: personalized labels

Apply handcrafted labels to your finished creations, on the inside, at the center-back neckline or on the facing at the closure. Sew labels in place with a few discreet stitches at each top corner. The example below was made by printing text on a strip of fabric, which was then appliquéd to another fabric—a print with sewing motifs—that was cut with pinking shears. The appliqué stitches are intentionally irregular.

Sequins

Use embroidery thread or doubled sewing thread. Attach sequins that have a center hole with one, two or three stitches, depending on the amount of movement you want them to have. One stitch is sufficient for attaching a sequin with an off-center hole. For either type, sew each one on individually, securing the thread on the wrong side of the work before attaching another one.

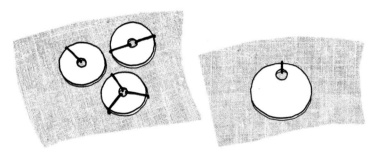

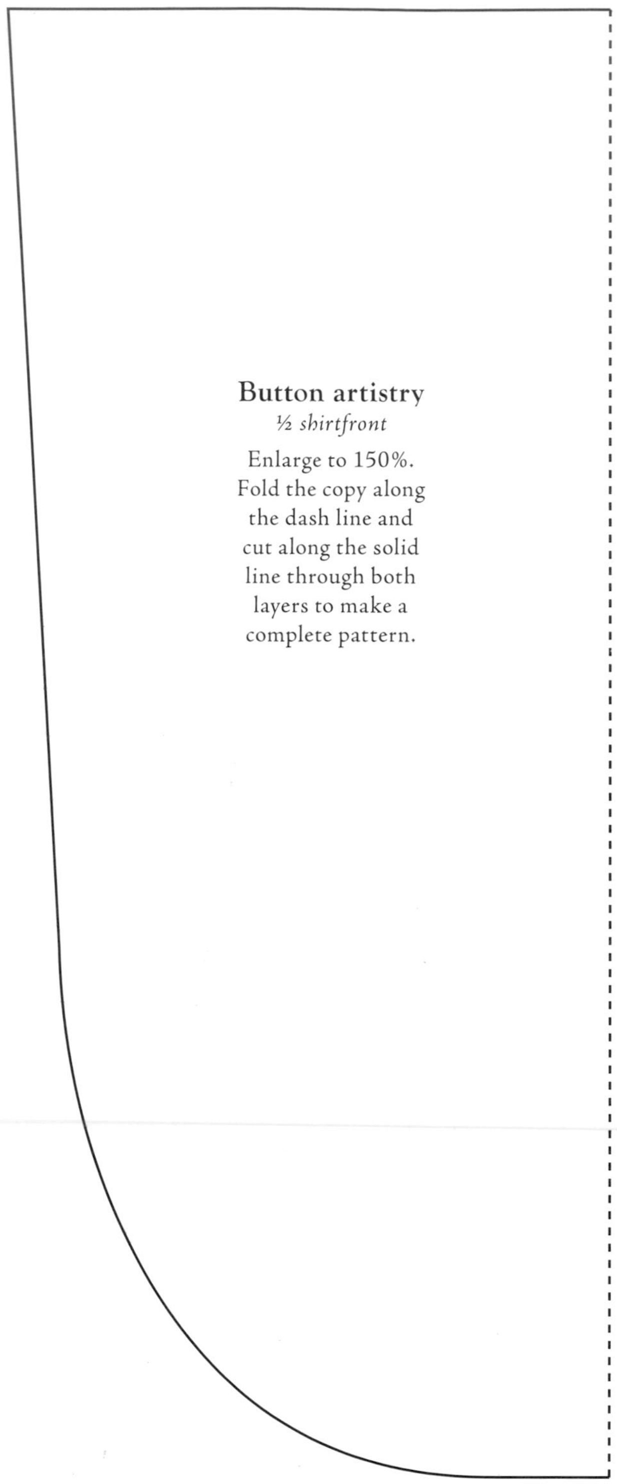

Button artistry
½ shirtfront

Enlarge to 150%.
Fold the copy along
the dash line and
cut along the solid
line through both
layers to make a
complete pattern.

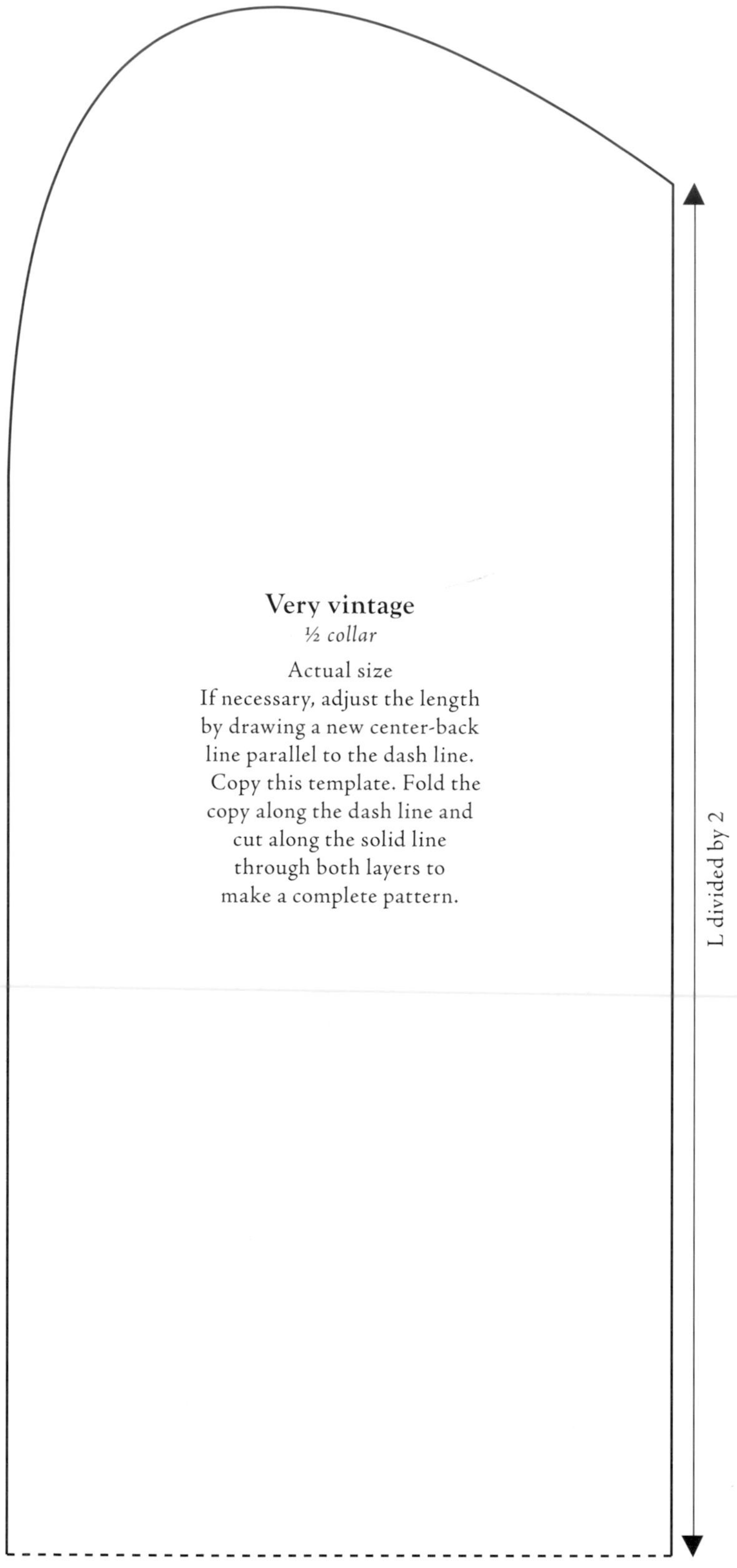

Very vintage
½ collar

Actual size
If necessary, adjust the length
by drawing a new center-back
line parallel to the dash line.
Copy this template. Fold the
copy along the dash line and
cut along the solid line
through both layers to
make a complete pattern.

L divided by 2

Latin Quarter tunic
Pocket
Actual size

Tip

Alway orient the pieces on the straight grain of your fabric. To do this, turn them as they will be placed on the garment and align their vertical edges (or the marked straight-grain line) parallel to the woven edge of the fabric.

This is especially important for large pieces like the overlays on the Twist Skirt. If these are not cut on the straight grain they may not hang correctly: they could be too tight or too loose. Either way, they could pucker disgracefully!

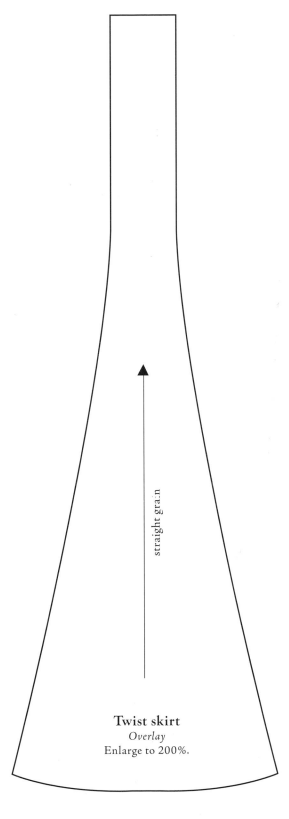

straight grain

Twist skirt
Overlay
Enlarge to 200%.

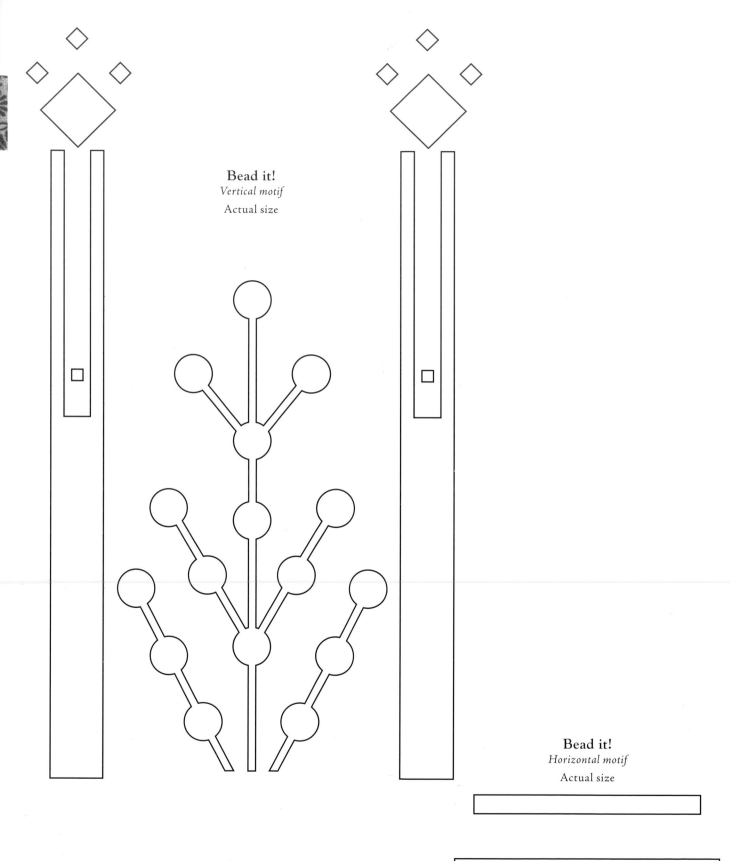

Bead it!
Vertical motif
Actual size

Bead it!
Horizontal motif
Actual size

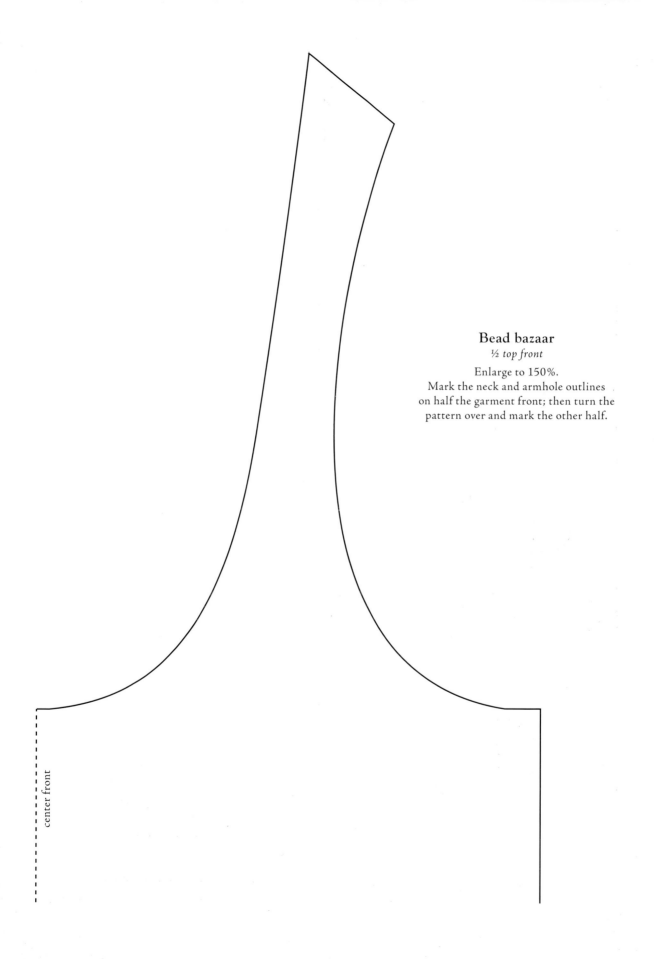

Bead bazaar
½ top front
Enlarge to 150%.
Mark the neck and armhole outlines
on half the garment front; then turn the
pattern over and mark the other half.

center front

Free spirit

Appliqués
Enlarge blue and yellow motifs to 200%

—— background motifs
—— top motifs

Flower 1
Actual size

Flower 2
Actual size

Flower 3
Actual size

Flower 4
Actual size

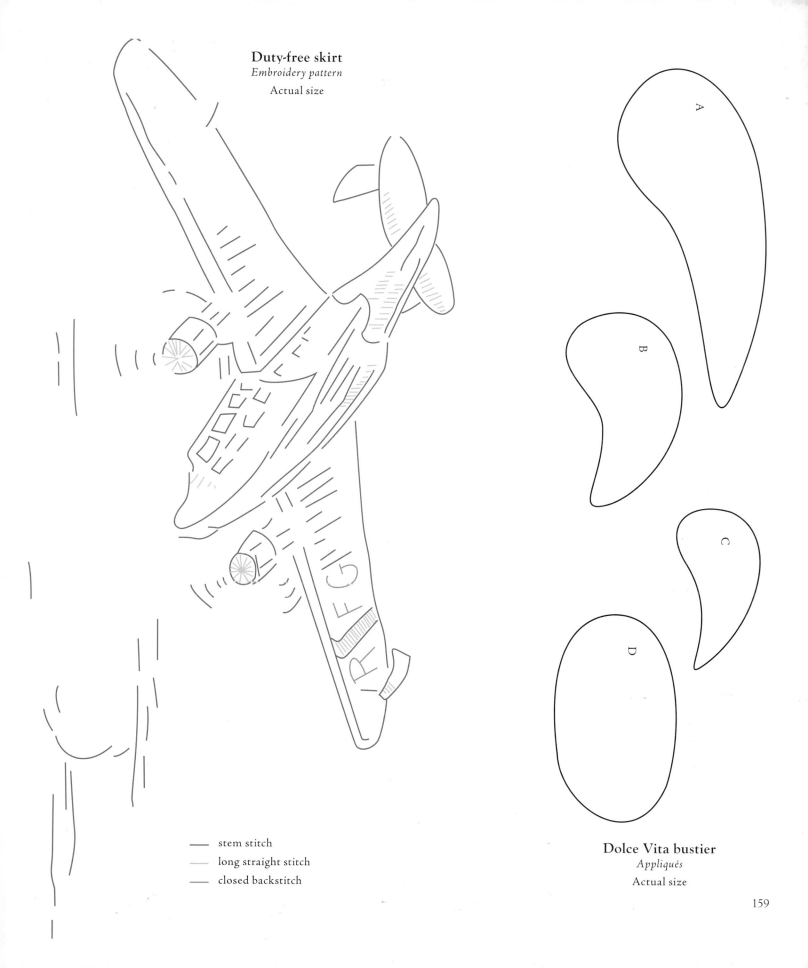

Duty-free skirt
Embroidery pattern
Actual size

stem stitch
long straight stitch
closed backstitch

Dolce Vita bustier
Appliqués
Actual size

Dolce Vita bustier
Appliqué placement guide
Enlarge to 200%